Come-On!
CENTS

Come-On! CENTS

Blueprint for Economic Recovery

Chris Murtagh

TATE PUBLISHING
AND ENTERPRISES, LLC

Published by Tate Publishing & Enterprises, LLC
127 E. Trade Center Terrace | Mustang, Oklahoma 73064 USA
1.888.361.9473 | www.tatepublishing.com

Tate Publishing is committed to excellence in the publishing industry. The company reflects the philosophy established by the founders, based on Psalm 68:11,
"The Lord gave the word and great was the company of those who published it."

Book design copyright © 2012 by Tate Publishing, LLC. All rights reserved.
Cover design by Erin DeMoss
Interior design by Chelsea Womble

Published in the United States of America

ISBN: 978-1-61862-735-3
Political Science / General
12.02.13

Addressed to the Shareholders of America on the following interesting subjects:

1. Grow America
2. America's Lost Prohibition Battle
3. Cell Solider
4. NOPEC
5. OBMD
6. The Prodigal Sum
7. I Can't Ability
8. $27 Trillion GDP in 2016

> Everywhere, man blames nature and fate, yet his fate is mostly but the echo of his character and passions, his mistakes and weaknesses.
>
> —Democritus (ca.460 BC-ca.370 BC)

DEDICATION

To my children Andrew and Christina who tire of my advice; my good friend Randy Robertson who sparked the concept of this book and to my wife, Polly who has patiently and lovingly supported me throughout my life; thank you.

CONTENTS

INTRODUCTION

*Come-on! Cent*s provides one perspective of today's world that challenges the decisions we, as Americans, make on a daily basis and measures those decisions from a business and economic perspective. The concept of *Come-On! Cents* is a satirical view of bits and pieces of everyday knowledge that we begrudgingly support, due to our lack of interest, data, and attention, or just simple acceptance of our way of life in today's world.

Different from pure satire, that tends not to provide a remedy, the story challenges those decisions with a business executive team that manages the company "1776, LLC," a unique business enterprise that supported the design of the American Constitution and provides an economic remedy to those more recent decisions made by its shareholders, the 310 million Americans. 1776 LLC has been in business since 1776 and was a guiding light for the Founding Fathers that persuaded those individuals to make bold and innovative decisions that eventually led to the creation of the America supported by the 1776, LLC business model.

These economic remedies, driven purely by 1776, LLC management team profit motives, look at our questionable past decisions, place a price tag on the costs of those decisions, and provide a remedy to put America back on its original business plan of freedom, prosperity, and sustainability.

As present day shareholders of 1776 LLC, Americans-all 310 Million of us-are responsible for the economic success or failures we have today, yet many of us do not reflect upon the decisions we made yesterday or make today that allow for these economic forces to come into play. Let's not blame the government (we voted for these guys and put them there), let's not blame the banks (they were there for us when we needed the cash), let's not blame the credit card companies, the auto loans, the home equity lines or fate; as these could all be avoided. The shareholders-all 310 million of us-need to understand that its shareholders maintain diligence over the decisions we make and link the longer term effect of these not simply from a moral or personal "feelings" perspective but combine those with economic and longer term sustainable effect. Without a balanced perspective, we find ourselves at the precipice of an economic meltdown turning each of us against each other and providing for class or race warfare by which previous societies have failed.

Seventeen seventy-six, LLC management team has reviewed these present-day dilemmas, reverted to decisions made in the past and present-day as its basis, and projects growing our present-day economy from $15 trillion to $25 trillion in just five years by challenging those decisions and projecting their financial impact on America's economy.

Seventeen seventy-six, LLC's management team is no different from any other USA business that seeks to grow and sustain its operations by reviewing its strengths, weaknesses, opportunities, and threats of its business model and finds that "we the people" have been at the very heart of these decisions and that "we the people" and not the government have the responsibility to face up to the present-day state of affairs. We either change the perspective by providing the economic power and entrepreneurial spirit that historically defined the creation and growth of 1776, LLC, or stay content in our current state of affairs and attempt to provide some prosperity for future generations that, at present day, appear reaching. *Come-on! Cents* provides bold and reaching solutions that are conceptual in their nature and are designed from a purely business perspective and attempt to eliminate the vacuum that nature abhors.

1776 EXECUTIVE MANAGEMENT TEAM MEETING: NOVEMBER 2011

CEO 1776, LLC: "Gentlemen the purpose of this meeting to get us back to the basics, look at where we have been, and try to find out what the hell is going on with our company. Our shareholders are at near-record level unemployment, treasury has exceeded their debt ceiling, we have little if any growth plans, and our basic infrastructure is crumbling. More importantly, what the heck are our 310 million shareholders doing?

"I need economic solutions, I need bold growth plans, and I want us to think back to the early days of our charter where we put bold yet effective plans in place, ran those British guys out of town, put together the basic components and designed one of the most creative business models ever introduced on the face of the earth. I want open discussions, everything is on the table."

Unlike publically traded global corporations, 1776 LLC management team is focused exclusively on the economic prosperity of a single market–the USA– with its goal to sustain its shareholder's liberty, freedom and future prosperity by challenging the economic status quo and designing bold and innovative solutions driving unprecedented change more typical of its Declaration of Independence efforts.

Its management team has seen the birth of a nation, Civil War, World Wars and a number of prudent and mismanaged global skirmishes that, in most cases, brought its shareholders together in a single focus responding to the challenges of the day and eventually reaping the benefits of a nation that believed in itself and its cause.

The executive team includes: VP Human Resources, VP Sales, VP Marketing, VP Business Development, VP Finance, VP Manufacturing and Operations and VP Research and Development who have all voiced concerns regarding the USA's lack of innovative growth and is upset with its present day lack of vision and direction. Each management team member had the opportunity to meet with their staff, gathering select information prior to the meeting, and each prepared to outline their views

Chris Murtagh

and opinions understanding that, after 235 years together, the final solutions would provide the direction needed to move 1776 LLC into economic prosperity.

The venue selected for 1776 LLC executive management meeting was the Green Valley Ranch Hotel located in Henderson Nevada one of the fastest growing cities in the United States during the Nevada boom years of 1980-2000 and a suburb of Las Vegas. The venue was appropriate for the team's discussions as Southern Nevada's unemployment topped the nation at approximately 14% with the majority of homes "underwater" and no clear innovative growth plans to provide economic prosperity for this once booming and innovative city. The meeting room, provided a popular "U" shaped seating arrangement, facing a ten foot by ten foot projector screen ready for each of the manager's overview's and presentations.

John Hearn, the CEO, a razor sharp finance and operations manager, was the main driver behind the development of the Declaration of Independence convincing the founding fathers to add to the declaration " And for the support of this Declaration, with a firm reliance on the protection of divine Providence, we mutually pledge to each other our Lives, our Fortunes and our sacred Honor." Hearn's ability to influence the document by having the new governing body pledge their lives and fortunes to its success elevated Hearn to the position of CEO for 1776 LLC, following the Declaration of Independence release in 1776.

CEO: HEARN: "As incredulous as it appears, gentlemen, the shareholders have withdrawn from depending upon their own talents and fortitude to lift them out of this economic crisis and increasingly depend upon the governing bodies to drive innovation and market forces. Many of our shareholders do not understand the individual power each one of them possess to drive these changes and tend to get lost in the chaos of these governing leaders who may tend to put their own personal gain ahead of the interests of our charter. Our government was not designed to define the market forces or drive innovation. The 1776 charter is to enhance individual efforts, provide an effective and balanced guideline for these innovations to flourish and provide an environment of freedom to support these economic drivers. I fear that we are moving towards an environment of significant government intervention and centralized thinking that tend to destroy innovation as most governing participants are not schooled in market forces and economic developments and tend to see the world from a different platform as compared to business investors and entrepreneurs. While we are still in the development stage of our young company-only 235 years old- I fear that unless we take bold steps in economic developments and take a hard look at the decisions made by these shareholders, we will not be able to sustain our longer term goals of freedom and liberty as we drive deeper and deeper into debt with no clear economic developments on the horizon and doom our company to the hands of fate. With that said, I look forward to our heated discussions and look to bold and innovative solutions from this management team; solutions that make sense to the shareholders with a clear reminder to these shareholders that they, the shareholders, are individually responsible for the present day economic turmoil and that they-the shareholders-are responsible for improving on this present day uncertainty. They need to use the power the forefathers gave to each of them to drive this change for their own personal freedoms, liberty and economic security that, when combined, support their pursuit of happiness. I look to a common sense approach with solutions that can be understood by all shareholders. Let us start with simple opening statements from each of you and get into the meat and potatoes as this develops."

Gene Gether, 1776 VP Business Development, an eloquent speaker with crisp knowledge of market drivers, statistics and business designs, had a unique ability to sort through complex issues, and provide innovative solutions balancing these economic factors with a blunt overview of successful and failing business designs. Gether rose to his position following the end of the Revolutionary War and assisted in developing the initial Constitution in 1787, design of Madison's Bill of Rights in 1789 and focused on the design of a clear business model that would sustain 1776 far beyond its initial years.

GETHER: "I'd like to address the team, first, by way of a general overview of what the business development team sees as a decline in our company's geographic growth over the years. From the late 1700's through late 1800's our company grew from the initial 13 colonies to what we know now as the geographic United States of America including the lower 48 states and the more recent acquisitions of

Hawaii and Alaska. Our country's expansion during its first 100 years rivaled any other country in history. Since 1860, or the past 150 years or so, we ceased any meaningful geographic expansion and focused on infrastructure. From the mid 1800's to mid-1900's we invested in infrastructure to connect these geographic acquisitions and provide roads, power plants, clean water and other investments providing interstate support systems allowing market forces to flourish. In line with that growth, we provided regulations and guidelines in which these businesses could flourish with an even playing field, were possible and practical, leading us to our present day business model. In order to accomplish these tasks, we designed a stronger Federal and centralized governing body to provide order and consistency to support this growth and level the playing field between the sovereign states."

"In addition to declining geographic expansion, our population growth has slowed significantly since our inception. As you can see from our first slide, 100 year population growth averaged over 30% from 1790-1880, declining to 20% growth every ten years from 1880-1910, declining to average of 15% every ten years from 1910-1970 with more sharp declines since 1970-2010 from 11% down to 7% in as recent as 2010."

Figure No: 1 USA Population Growth
1790-2010 US Census Bureau [1]

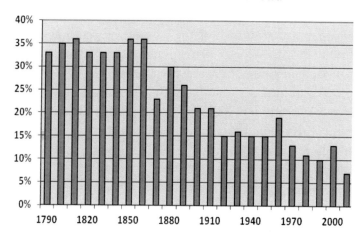

"The decline in population growth along with no recent geographic expansion provides a very difficult business scenario. In the founding first 100 years, these shareholders experienced rapid geographic and population increases that provided for the consumption of goods and services. We had hoped for continued growth following the baby-boomers born with their peak in the 1960's but due to decisions made by the shareholders in the 1970's, the ten year growth rates have declined considerably. Our plans to reverse these shareholder decisions are outlined in the more detailed

1   US Census Bureau Population Growth 1790-2010 http://www.census.gov/newsroom/releases/pdf/cb10-ffse02.pdf

presentations to follow. From a growth perspective, however, the basics appear quite simple. We have ceased all geographic expansions since 1860 and we have reduced the average ten year population growth of the base of the consumers from around 30% in 1790-1890 to around 10% in 2010 for overall growth reduction of 66% every ten years."

"We address the solution to this dilemma in the balance of our meeting but wanted to provide this opening statement with the understanding that in business, as in life, you are either growing or dying. The data seems to support the ladder."

Brian Young, VP Manufacturing and Operations, a hard headed innovative leader provided guidance to the management team and shareholders during the USA's manufacturing and expansion boom from its growth in cotton in the 1800's through its manufacturing boom of the late 1800-1950's where USA manufacturing innovation and expertise provided absorption of its manufacturing products on a global basis. Young's ability to understand the value added components of a manufacturing based economy and communicate those factors provided Young with a high degree of trust from his colleagues.

YOUNG: "Thanks Gene. As we all know and all understand, the shareholders have decided to move from a manufacturing driven economy to an economy driven by the service sector. We needed guidelines to reduce pollution and reduce employer related abuse of its employees and introduced collective bargaining unions to protect the interests of the workers and provide for a higher quality of products manufacturered in the USA. These changes did not come easily and provided a higher level of costs for our manufacturered goods. It was only a matter of time when developing nations would eventually take a portion of our global share of USA manufactured goods and services. In addition, during the 1970-1990's our leading automotive businesses got goofy providing inferior products and poor customer service and invited German and Japanese higher quality goods and services into the USA markets for which they are still paying the price today. In many cases, these international companies entered the US markets, built plants and products at higher quality and better customer service and are now on our shores reaping the benefits of previous poor decisions made by our shareholders. The basic commodity businesses including steel, plastics, clothing, furniture and a host of other businesses are now lost to China and will eventually be divided between China and India as those economies continue to offer lower prices at similar quality. Our first slide outlines manufacturing as a % of GDP from 1980-2008 showing USA manufacturing declining from about 22% in 1980 to approximately 12% in 2008.

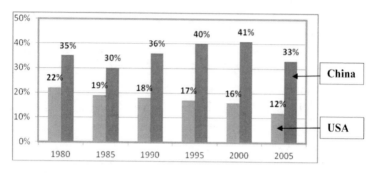

"Global manufacturing as a % of GDP tends to favor China who took advantage of lower labor costs and significant investments in manufacturing facilities and since 1985 has been the world leader in manufacturing as a per cent of their GDP. We expect the USA to continue its declining manufacturing base unless acted upon. As you all know, I do not favor poorly devised government tariffs, government intervention or other means of controlling imported goods unless there is proof of unfair trading practices. Apparently those exist with regards to China but the shareholders have decided not act or react to those claims and in doing so further support that decline in manufacturing.

"As Gene mentioned earlier in his summary, we too have a solution to this dilemma and will present those in a case by case basis as we move forward later in our discussions."

2   Curious Cat Investing and Economics http://investing.curiouscat blog.net/2010/06/28/manufacturing-output-as-a-percent-of-gdp-by-country/

HEARN: "One question Brian, it appears Germany is slowly increasing its manufacturing as a % of GDP since 1995 and one of the only major economies to do so, any insight here?"

YOUNG: "In 2005, Germany introduced a series of reforms summarized in their "Agenda 2010" that basically reduced unemployment benefits, relaxed regulatory practices and reduced union wages. In addition it invested in smaller manufacturing enterprises better known as "Middlestand" that tend to put a higher priority on employing local citizens for these mostly privately held businesses. The combination of cost controls along with reduced regulatory practices and a sense of German loyalty for local employment appear to be the business model that has assisted Germany in increasing its manufacturing contributions to GDP.

HEARN: "Thanks Brian."

"What we have so far is declining USA population growth from around 30% every ten years in our early history to around 10% now, no geographic expansion of territories for the past 150 years or so, declining manufacturing contribution to GDP and shareholders who have decided to allow these phenomenon to take place. Robert, can you shake us loose from these otherwise sobering details and offer some highlights that provide some upside?"

Robert Blackwell, 1776 LLC's VP Human Resources regards the shareholders as the backbone of the company and has been amazed by their resiliency over the years through the creation of a nation, to civil war, world wars and tremendous growth that outpaced any other nation in terms of economic output and absorption. Blackwell's addition to the management team followed after the conclusion of the Civil War where widespread reconstruction efforts and elimination of slavery required significant changes to the Charter's human resource outlook and update of its constitution. Blackwell was a major influence in those areas and provides ongoing advice to the management team regarding the shareholder's human resource capabilities.

BLACKWELL: "From Minute Men to the soldiers in Iraq and Afghanistan, from slavery to civil rights, from several colonies to the greatest and most powerful nation in the world, our shareholders have risen to any challenge and have overcome great obstacles all for the sake of a lifestyle not offered by any other country in the world. John, I can offer some upside by communicating to the group that no matter the size or boldness of the plan we develop here -that plan is useless unless it can be executed. There is no better citizenry or better qualified body of people to execute a bold and innovative plan than our shareholders. The good news is that they can do just about anything if they are convinced it will lead to their pursuit of happiness and maintain their liberty and freedoms. The bad news is they are aging and at a rapid pace. I trust the spirit is willing and wonder if the body is capable. My difficulty is getting inside the heads of

Chris Murtagh

these existing shareholders and understanding what drives their spirit and what drives their desire to achieve greatness. In times of threat to the country, the shareholders tend to embrace each other for a common purpose and cause. "

"My opening slides take a look at the capabilities of these shareholders from the point of an aging society, education, well being and access the human spirit readiness of this group of shareholders along with their ability to execute a bold recovery plan." Figure No 3shows the growth rate of the USA labor force declining from annual growth rate of 2.5% in 1965 to "0" growth in 2015.

Figure No: 3 Annual Growth Rate of the U.S. Labor Force [3]

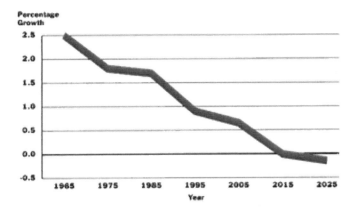

---

3   USA Social Security Administration

"In addition to declining labor force growth rates, the average age of the USA employed person has increased from 34.5 years old in 1980 to 41.5 years old in 2010.

Figure No: 4 Age of US Average Labor Force Age[4]

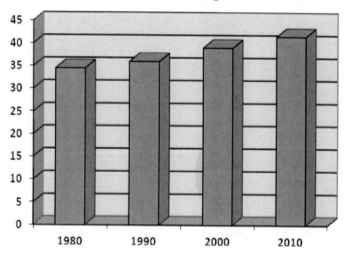

"Figures No 3&4 are compelling as they tell the story of a declining growth in the labor force and an increase in the labor force age. We have tracked this back to decisions made by the shareholders during the 1970's that have a direct effect on what we now see today. We need then to expand your overview, John, as follows:

---

4   January/February 2008 Federal Reserve Bank of St Louis *Review*

"What we have so far is declining USA population growth from around 30% every ten years in our early history to around 10% now, no geographic expansion of territories for the past 150 years or so, declining manufacturing contribution to GDP and shareholders who have decided to allow these phenomenons to take place. In addition, the workforce that grew at an annual rate of 2.5% in 1965 has declined to a forecast zero growth in 2015 and its workforce aging from 34.5 years old in 1980 to 41.5 years old in 2010 or 20% increase in labor force age over the past 30 years."

"I feel that we have time to make bold changes but need to do so sooner than later since the data appears to be working against us in our physical ability to rebound from these phenomenons.

HEARN: "Robert, for my own curiosity, what was the make-up of the workforce in earlier times?"

BLACKWELL: "With regards to age, the data is difficult to assimilate due to a large number of younger workers employed in the 1900-1940's below the age of 16 years old but our best guess is that the average labor force age sine the 1950's is somewhere between 36-38 years old. Data prior to the 1900's included a larger percentage of agricultural workers-many family owned businesses-which we feel are less relevant to these discussions. With regards to male and female ratios we find a significant increase in female workers.

Let me provide Figure No: 5 for consideration. According to the US Department of Labor Statistics, women in the workforce have grown from 5.3 Million in 1900 to slightly over 72 Million in 2010."

Figure No: 5 Women in the US Workforce (thou) 1900-2010[5]

"Today approximately 60% of all eligible women over the age of 16 are employed. Men make up slightly higher than 50% of today's workforce with approximately 75% of eligible men over the age of 16 employed. Our last slide, Figure No: 5 show the overall change since 1890.

_____

5   US Department of Labor-Women's Bureau

Figure No: 6 US Labor Force Participation Rate by Gender 1890-1990[6]

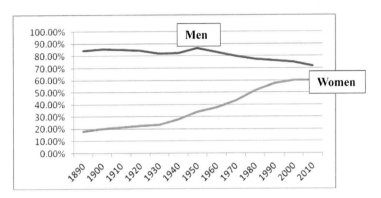

HEARN: "If I understand the data correctly women have been the fastest growing contributor to the workforce with men declining mostly since 1950. Well thank goodness for the American women."

6   Labor force participation by gender of U.S. residents, 1890–1990. Source: Blau, Ferber, and Winkler (2002, table 4.1). Participation rates pertain to the total population prior to 1950 and the civilian population thereafter. Data include individuals 14 years of age prior to 1950 and 16+years thereafter. http://www.bls.gov/opub/ted/2007/jan/wk2/art03.htm

BLACKWELL: "If I may add to the summary statement:

> "What we have so far is declining USA population growth from around 30% every ten years in our early history to around 10% now, no geographic expansion of territories for the past 150 years or so, declining manufacturing contribution to GDP and shareholders who have decided to allow these phenomenon's to take place. In addition, the workforce that grew at an annual rate of 2.5% in 1965 has declined to a forecast zero growth in 2015 and its workforce is aging from an average of 34.5 years old in 1980 to 41.5 years old in 2010 or 20% increase in labor force age over the past 30 years. In addition, women are the fastest growing contribution to the shareholder's workforce since 1950 where in today's world 60% of eligible women are employed as compared to 18% in 1890."

As is the case with any business, management's role is to understand its available resources both financial and human, prior to recommending any changes, especially bold and innovative ones, to ensure the participants are capable of executing and sustaining a meaningful and longer lasting change. The previous decisions made by these shareholders lead us to where we are today and are reviewed in the following chapters; their purpose to provide an understanding of where we are today, how we got here and solutions to remedy these past decisions.

HEARN: "Technology and their enterprise play an important role in supporting any changes that you guys are preparing to recommend. Sam, give us a perspective on our global leadership with regards to our technological readiness and capabilities so we can plan effectively."

Samuel Thorpe, 1776LLC's VP Research and Development held degrees in physics, engineering, math and biological sciences, and a great supporter of technology and its effect on the economy. From the cotton gin that revolutionized the cotton industry, electricity, streamlined manufacturing, software development, transportation and infrastructure and, more recently, the biotechnical developments, Sam often prodded governing agencies and industry leaders to reach far beyond their capabilities in a logistical manner to develop new methods, products and approaches to support continued prosperity of American companies.

THORPE: "I did not know that women's contribution to our shareholder's prosperity was that great. Thank you for that Brian, I really did not know that. Gentlemen, we have all labored under this recent and unacceptable economic weight that unfortunately has us and the world by the throat.

"Unfortunately or fortunately, I care only about our shareholders and can provide, in my opening statement, my assessment of their readiness and capabilities, as I see them. I limit my discussions to the technological advances we would like to make and will propose certain solutions later in these discussions. Let me start off with some very basic components, as I see it, for our plan. There are the doers, the thinkers and the support systems where the support systems contributors function is to control, regulate, litigate and measure their actions and success. I see a significant increase in the latter, specifically the support system component, that will need to be addressed during our discussions as they are playing an increasing role in the shareholders ability or inability to create value. I do not wish to undermine these support system components, but wish to clarify that they support and not lead innovation, and that their actions do not hinder the doers and the thinkers and, in addition, we design those support services to enlighten and enhance the efforts of those doers and thinkers and not distract them from their goals."

"Are the shareholders of this magnificent experiment called the Unites States of America ready? Do they have the fortitude, wisdom, understanding, council and knowledge to succeed? And more importantly, are they willing to invest and believe in a common cause? I feel, with some reluctance, that yes, these shareholders are ready and more importantly, have the heart to overcome any obstacle as they have a unique knowledge of freedom that no other country offers. My reluctance is not in the shareholder's desire to support the plans we are about to recommend. My reluctance is in the support structure's ability to be controlled, peeled back and be ready to support these shareholders as we introduce one of the boldest growth concepts ever undertaken that rivals China's recent 10-15 year economic developments.

"My first slide outlines our educational readiness and provides an overview of where we are now and where we need to be to support any meaningful change. I suggest we keep in mind that during the development of our growth plan, the support structure, mentioned above, will be reluctant to provide a subordinated position to the doers and thinkers unless the plan has merit and unless they can contribute. The table before you is the shareholder's present day educational rank level at "14" or about average. I am most disturbed regarding math's rating at "25" and science rating at "17". Technological leadership requires a much higher rating in science and math yet the shareholders tolerate the level of education they receive now. While in the past I was less concerned about the situation, we now have to compete with smarter and better prepared global competitors. These test results were for sampled for 15 year old students and not simply overall grammar school test samples.

Table No: 1 USA 2009 Global Education Rating [7]
OECD Country Ratings

Rank	Reading	Math	Science
1	S. Korea	S. Korea	Finland
2	Finland	Finland	Japan
3	Canada	Japan	S. Korea
4	New Zealand	Switzerland	New Zealand
5	Japan	Japan	Canada
6	Australia	Netherlands	Estonia
7	Netherlands	New Zealand	Australia
8	Belgium	Belgium	Netherlands
9	Norway	Australia	Germany
10	Estonia	Germany	Switzerland

---

7   OECD 2009 Database: Ranking within OECD Countries Only

11	Switzerland	Estonia	UK
12	Poland	Iceland	Slovenia
13	Iceland	Denmark	Poland
14	USA	Slovenia	Ireland
15	Sweden	Norway	Belgium
16	Germany	France	Hungary
17	Ireland	Slovakia	USA
18	France	Austria	Czech Republic
19	Denmark	Poland	Norway
20	UK	Sweden	Denmark
21	Hungary	Czech Republic	France
22	Portugal	UK	Iceland
23	Italy	Hungary	Sweden
24	Slovenia	Luxemburg	Austria
25	Greece	USA	Portugal
26	Spain	Ireland	Slovakia
27	Czech Republic	Portugal	Italy
28	Slovakia	Spain	Spain
29	Israel	Italy	Luxemburg
30	Luxemburg	Greece	Greece

"If the growth plans that we are about to propose are in areas that require significant technological developments where we are required to sustain technological leadership, than no; the shareholders are ill prepared for the future. If our economic developments are focused on less highly technological advancements, then I say the doers and not the thinkers will rule the day as long as we can reverse the power the support structure takes in controlling the doers. The shareholder's allow for a high school completion rate at 25% and that varies by individual state. My second slide reviews the actual graduation rates by state. Let's face it gentlemen, these shareholder's are not prepared for tomorrow's technological leadership. My second slide, Figure Number 7, shows the graduation rates of entering high school students as of 2009 that averaged slightly less than 76%.

Chris Murtagh

Figure No: 7 Average USA Freshman Graduation Rates 2008-2009[8]

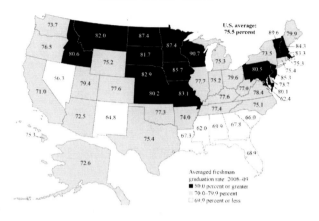

HEARN: "Sam, I appreciate the metrics and your comments. The shareholder's however are seen as technological leaders on a global basis today. Are you suggesting that any improvement plans we devise not include technology leadership? I have a problem with that."

THORPE:" I felt it prudent to outline the basic components that will sustain the development plans we are about to consider and that, in my opinion, the shareholder's are not prepared to sustain any technological leadership given

---

8   Trends in High School and Drop out Completion Rates United States: 1972-2009....US Department of Education IES: 2012-006-National Center for Educational Statistics

the basic educational systems that are in place today. While these shareholders may have provided technology leadership in the information age, the products are easily copied or manufactured off shore. While biotechnologies will drive new innovations and the shareholders is a leading contributor, they are not **the** leading contributor and as time moves forward they do not have the basic tools on a national level to sustain. My concerns John are to ensure that the team appreciates the capabilities these shareholders have and not weigh too heavily on technology leadership as its driving force for change."

The dialogue between Hearn and Thorpe has the team intrigued. On one hand investment in technology has historically driven changes in economic output, redefined wars and had always been a major component in any economic turnaround. Careful not to disrupt their colleague's opening statement yet emotionally charged by the dialogue and baseline information, Blackwell-the teams VP Human Resources see's an opening in the pause between Thorpe and Ahearn and ceases the opportunity.

BLACKWELL: "Gentlemen, we are at an interesting point in our discussions that I feel will lead us down the road so many times traveled by the shareholder's support groups that look to the heaven's for solutions to their educational infrastructure. I feel Sam has provided us with critical information that, no doubt, will require the team to keep that information in perspective as we move forward. I might add that there is a metric missing from the data that has often times been miscalculated from an educational perspective. Recent developments from Steve Jobs and Bill Gates, both college dropouts led the shareholders into global expansion; Thomas Edison had little formal grammar school education and was schooled by his mother. The list goes on and on.

THORPE: "I agree. But eventually these entrepreneurs hired competent educated people to execute their innovative ideas. I do not disagree that the shareholders obtain a great entrepreneur spirit, they do. However, the world is catching up with our shareholder's spirit; and catching up quite rapidly."

BLACKWELL: "Point taken!"

HEARN: "Sam, how does this academic rating compare historically?

THORPE:"Comparing the shareholders overall reading competencies, the category where the shareholders scored the highest, I include my third slide-figure number eight. Competencies in reading, as an example, have been on the decline since 1993."

Figure No: 8 17 Year Old USA Average Reading Scale Score 1971-2004[9]

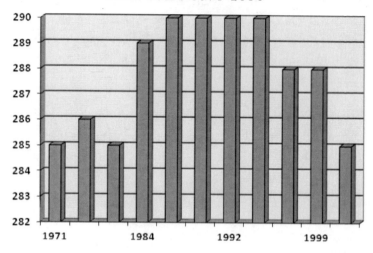

HEARN: "Ok. I've seen enough. Thanks Sam."

THORPE: "My pleasure, John. Moving ahead with the team's overall opening statements and John's early summary let me add to the observation the following:

9   U.S. Department of Education, National Center for Education Statistics, National Assessment of Educational Progress (NAEP), NAEP 2004 Trends in Academic Progress; and NAEP Data Explorer (http://nces.ed.gov/nationsreportcard/nde/), retrieved January 2006. (This table was prepared February 2006.)

"What we have so far is declining USA population growth from around 30% every ten years in our early history to around 10% now, no geographic expansion of territories for the past 150 years or so, declining manufacturing contribution to GDP and shareholders who have decided to allow these phenomenon's to take place. In addition, the workforce that grew at an annual rate of 2.5% in 1965 has declined to a forecast zero growth in 2015 and its workforce is aging from an average of 34.5 years old in 1980 to 41.5 years old in 2010 or 20% increase in labor force age over the past 30 years. In addition, women are the fastest growing contribution to the shareholder's workforce since 1950 where in today's world 60% of eligible women are employed as compared to 18% in 1890. From a future growth perspective, the shareholder's global educational system has been downgraded to "average" ranked overall 14th in the global economy, and its reading levels have not changed materially since 1971."

"Marketing has always been a funny science. Many of our shareholders view this as simple advertising or how to position a product or service. Some view marketing as simple as finding a need and filling that need with a product or service."

Mike Brinster, the VP Marketing, stepped to the front of the room as he signaled his colleagues that now the brilliance of marketing was about to be unveiled upon the team. Brinster an astute marketer and popular with his colleagues has a unique flavor of market forces, consumer needs, driving trends and could provide unique "models" to forecast the effect of these driving influences in such a way as to bring peace and calm to the group by providing direction.

"Marketing", said Brinster "is everything!"

BRINSTER: "Thank you Sam, I think the overview regarding education cannot be undermined. What is it that our shareholders do every day and what is it about America that drives it to such a successful conclusion regardless of the calamity it faces? Compared to the Civil War or World Wars, this economic relapse is a bump in the road. I agree it's a significant bump, but I feel we needed this to shake the shareholders into reality. As a matter of opinion, I feel the shareholders needed this kick in the butt to get them motivated. I love growth, I enjoy the challenge of changing the playing field and I especially enjoy doing it with these shareholders.

"They all knew manufacturing was declining, they knew certain countries were taking advantage of labor and pricing practices and they knew the educational system was one leading to eventual mediocrity and here we are today all looking at slides and support information that was basically foretold years ago."

"Let's look at the powerhouse our company is on a global basis and what differentiates 1776 LLC, our company, from the rest of the world. The shareholders are the consumers of world products at a blistering pace. These individual shareholders out consume any other country and, as the world's leading consumer, have tremendous power that the shareholders do not use or do not understand. In addition, freedom, liberty and pursuit of happiness are clear differentiators these shareholders have that are the envy of the global markets. My opening statements are limited to these two differentiators. Figure Number 9 on the screen, outlines shareholder consumption of goods and services it imports, for this example, from China-those dollars are projected at slightly less than $400 Billion by year ending 2011. The shareholders exports however are projected at slightly less than $100 Billion in 2011 leaving a deficient with China of approximately $300 Billion in 2011 alone. In 1985 imports and exports to and from China were approximately $4 Billion in imports from China to the USA and $4 Billion in exports from the USA to China with no deficit between the countries.

Figure No: 9 USA and China Trade Balance 1985-2010[10]

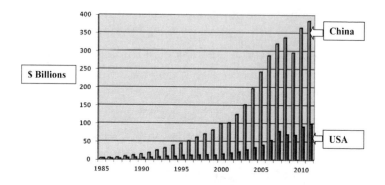

"If you add up the deficits between the USA and China, China imported goods of $3.4 Trillion dollars from 1985-2011 into the US and the US exported only $736 Billion in that same period to China for a 15 year deficient of approximately $2.7 Trillion dollars. The forecast of China imports in 2011 is approximately $400 Billion. For USA companies, who average around $200,000 per employee in manufacturing productivity, you are looking at 2 million manufacturing jobs gone in 2011 alone to China. I want to thank Brian and the guys in manufacturing that helped me in putting this information together and it paints two pictures. One picture is what the heck are these shareholders thinking with regards to exporting so many jobs, but I'll leave that to Brian and the

---

10   US Census Bureau http://www.census.gov/foreign-trade/balance/c5700.html

manufacturing guys. The other picture is the USA shareholder consumption of these China manufacturered goods and how dependent the Chinese are in their continuing to absorb China products. The USA consumer, our shareholders, really does not care where the product was made as long as the value proposition is there. In addition, if a 14 year old minor can crank out plastic cups in China at a fraction of the cost the shareholders can accomplish with the shareholder's modern plants and factories, perhaps the shareholders need to remove themselves from that business. If on the other hand China is not playing fairly, then the support services group mentioned earlier needs to step in and correct that-but they have chosen not to do so. "

"Given the reluctance of the support group to remedy the playing field, the doers and thinkers need to bring about market changes to affect the situation. We intend on expanding on that in the next several hours, but wanted to highlight this in my opening remarks."

"The second item that differentiates the shareholder's business model is freedom, liberty and the pursuit of happiness. While there is no overhead slide I can provide to you to support the practicality of our shareholders lifestyle, I submit that our marketing plans will focus on that lifestyle as a competitive edge against global competition and I intend to leverage that in the growth plans we discuss today. We have around 4.4% of the global population share or 310 million of the 7 Billion inhabitants. I propose we increase that share over the next 7 years to 400 Million or around 5.6% global share and take share from the overall markets by importing select highly educated consumers into the USA and expanding our consumer base by 80 Million over the next 5 years or around 16 million per year. The details of that plan will be outlined following these opening remarks. I submit we cannot compete with these lower overseas manufacturing costs and instead of trying to export products we import consumers."

BLACKWELL: "Mike, I think you have set an interesting tone. Our freedom's and quality of life come at high costs. To the credit of the shareholder's support group, these ongoing regulations ensure a certain quality of life, but they are not free and come at a high cost. Importing over 80 Million consumers into the USA is bold and I like it!

YOUNG: "In addition, I would add that we tweak the services and support group (especially the government services team) to do something about those unfair trading practices and balance your growth plans with practical trading rules. If not, I would have the shareholders up in arms and break the back of these unfair trading practices and have them "Occupy China" or "Occupy the White House" until this is turned around."

GETHER: "Easy guys. A trade war, now-in this environment? Humm-could be interesting if it were sparked by the shareholders and not the government. If the shareholders really knew that this level of imbalance existed between the countries, they may drive boycotts, demand producers publish % of foreign components that are used in their end product or any other combination of shareholder discontent pulling power from the government groups into the hands of the consumers. Powerful, yes Brian, very powerful. I think Ben Franklin would have a chuckle on that one.

The last of the management team's opening remarks were about to be heard. While Brinster hinted at some upcoming bold marketing initiatives elevating the group's spirit, the group knew that the bartender, VP of Finance, was about to ask for "last call" and flicker the dreaded lights providing a more sobering set of financials.

Jeff Darbon, 1776's VP Finance, was a cracker-jack finance wizard, schooled at the leading finance institutions of their day and was a hand on operations type manager that linked the supply and demand market challenges to the company financials.

DARBON: "Great overview Mike. I agree that marketing is key and look forward to working with each of you in providing the most aggressive and bold plan to turn this debt written economy into a sustaining powerhouse that adds to the economic freedom's that each of our shareholders aspires to. I'm not going to dwell on the financial affairs as we all agree they are in dismal condition. My opening statements and overviews really are a measure of where we have been and the price we are paying today for those decisions made by the shareholders in the past.

"Two areas I would like to dwell on include our national debt and a 30 year look back on where we have spent the tax payer's money."

"The support group that was outlined earlier when Brian brought up the doers, thinkers and support group categories tend to include governing officials, lawyers, finance people and others that do not necessarily create value in the goods and services side but do add value in keeping the operations folks (doers and thinkers) abreast of the actual financial results and should be providing a level playing field for the shareholders. From the governing portion of the support group, I have to concur with the team that the governing support services group have moved from a flexible state by state management system to a highly centralized one creating increasing regulations and bureaucracy that tend to infringe on those shareholders liberties and pursuit of happiness. Then again, it is the shareholders that put these individuals in power and therefore it is the shareholders that carry the burden of their decisions."

"My opening comments are focused on the shareholder's debt and GDP (Gross Domestic Product) growth that are both the topics of major debates with the shareholders today. On one hand certain members in government wish to increase debt and pay for entitlement programs it can't afford, borrowing large sums of money with only "hope" as its longer term plan to pay down the debt. That action will burden future shareholders, many that are not even born now, with repayment of that debt and interest over the years. On the other hand, there exists a group in the government firmly committed to reducing spending and reducing the debt eliminating support programs and committed to little or no increase in taxes. Neither side has any growth plans or policies with most posturing every four years for re-election. The shareholders sit on the sidelines; major corporations wait out their special interests and increasing government regulations pour out of every facet of congress. The old "let's repair the infrastructure arguments" are at play again and will eventually fizzle or be mismanaged as is the case with most government intervention. In addition the weight of, "let's reduce the tax burden" arguments are stagnating the air they breathe further confusing and baffling the shareholders. This is where the support group fails. It fails in not educating the shareholder's effectively and placing poorly designed options before them, chaos and confusion, followed by finger pointing and blame are the results."

"Directing your attention to the screen my first slide, table number 2, combines local, state and federal spending from 1970 through 2010.

Table No: 2 US Government Spending ($Billions) 1970-2010 Federal, State and Local [11]

Category	1970	1980	1990	2000	2010	Growth
Defense	$95	$168	$342	$359	$848	793%
% Growth		78%	104%	5%	136%	
Pensions	$31	$143	$305	$544	$939	2930%
% Growth		361%	194%	78%	73%	
Healthcare	$22	$87	$224	$470	$1028	4572%
% Growth		295%	158%	103%	119%	
Education	$56	$152	$305	$543	$887	1483%
% Growth		171%	78%	78%	63%	
Welfare	$22	$101	$175	$294	$727	3205%
% Growth		360%	73%	68%	147%	
Protection	$8	$24	$54	$193	$312	3800%
% Growth		200%	125%	257%	62%	
Transportation	$22	$57	$104	$167	$271	1132%
% Growth		159%	82%	60%	62%	
General Govt.	$7	$32	$56	$70	$111	1485%
% Growth		357%	75%	25%	59%	
Other	$36	$95	$234	$294	$382	961%
% Growth		164%	146%	26%	30%	
Interest	$19	$67	$234	$293	$296	1457%
% Growth		252%	324%	120%	1%	
Balance	$4	$14	$56	$13	-$4	(100%)
% Growth		250%	300%	-77%	-130%	
Total Spend	**$322**	**$940**	**$2100**	**$3250**	**$5800**	1701%
% Growth		192%	123%	55%	78%	
Population	**203**	**226**	**248**	**281**	**310**	53%
% Growth		11%	10%	13%	10%	

11   http://www.usgovernmentspending.com/budget_pie_gs.php?span=usgs302&year=2010&view=1&expand=&expandC=&units=b&fy=fy12&local=undefined&state=US#usgs302

"Spending from local, state and federal government increased over 1700% during this timeframe with population increasing at around 53%. What is most startling is the spending in areas of growth that favor pensions, healthcare, protection and welfare-all non growth interests. The smaller areas of investment over this period include: transportation, education and defense all areas of investment for the future. With our infrastructure crumbling and our education rating declining to rank number 14 in the world, it should be no surprise that these shareholders find themselves in this predicament. My recommendations to reverse these areas of investment over the next five years are included in the balance of the presentation to be made by the team later in our meetings. Over the same period the population grows at about 10% every ten years with expenses growing at between 55% and 192% every ten years."

"Keep in mind spending includes all government agencies and not simply the Federal government. I argue that education, transportation and defense are all "investment" areas as these sustain and support the lifestyle and growth. The other categories areas of healthcare, pension and welfare are "expense areas" and a result of entitlements provided to the shareholders by their elected officials and do not secure growth or sustain lifestyles unless they can be afforded.

"My second group of slides, Figure No: 9A-9D shows the federal debt since 2006 and that debt as a % of GDP along with government forecasts through 2016. The debt has ballooned from $10 trillion on 2008 (Slide 9A) to forecast $16.7 Trillion in 2012 for a 67% increase in just 4 years Slide 9B shows our debt as a % of GDP slightly over 100%. Slide 9C compares this debt as a % of GDP from 1900 through 2011 with slide 9D the Federal debt since the inception of 1776 LLC. From slide number 9D we suggest that they are approaching the debt ratio seen during World War 2 with a history of declining investments and increasing expenses. I find these slides quite sobering!"

Slide No: 9A   Slide No: 9B

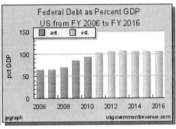

Slide No: 9C   Slide No: 9D

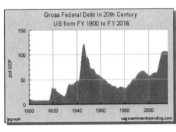
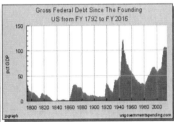

"With regards to the income or revenue drivers we look to the gross domestic product (GDP) and its historical influence. Slide No 10A provides an overview of GDP growth since 1947 around the end of World War 2. Slide No: 10 B provides the GDP annual growth in the same period. Slide 10B suggests shareholder GDP growth rates has been declining since around 1985 or so. I think the $2.7 Trillion deficient with China since 1985, that the marketing and manufacturing guys showed us earlier, are a contributing factor, but not the only factor."

Figure No: 10A USA Gross Domestic Product

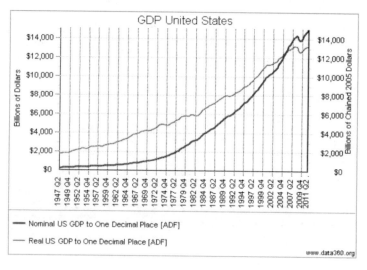

Figure No: 10B Gross Domestic Product Growth Rate

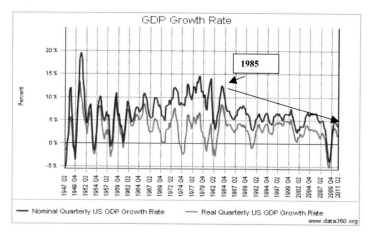

"That concludes my opening remarks. Let me add to that, if I can, that debt serves a good purpose if it supports investments or defense as both secure our freedoms, liberty and pursuit of happiness. Debt, without growth investments, is an ongoing burden that will not sustain our lifestyle. I concur with the group that bold plans are required to remedy this folly.

HEARN: "Jeff, the news while sobering, does give us a platform to start with. Let me then summarize these observations in the following overview to set the tone of the balance of our discussions:"

"What we have so far is declining USA population growth from around 30% every ten years in our early history to around 10% now, no geographic expansion of territories for the past 150 years or so, declining manufacturing contribution to GDP and shareholders who have decided to allow this phenomenon's to take place. In addition, the workforce that grew at an annual rate of 2.5% in 1965 has declined to a forecast zero growth in 2015 and its workforce is aging from an average of 34.5 years old in 1980 to 41.5 years old in 2010 or 20% increase in labor force age over the past 30 years. In addition, women are the fastest growing contribution to the shareholder's workforce since 1950 where in today's world 60% of eligible women are employed as compared to 18% in 1890. From a future growth perspective, the shareholder's global educational system has been downgraded to "average" ranked overall 14th in the global economy, and its reading levels have not changed materially since 1971. Our gross domestic product that grew at rates of between 8-15% since the end of World War 2 has been in decline since 1985 growing at rates of 3-5% driven any number of items with suggestions of manufacturing declines driven by the trade imbalance since 1985 with China dooming the shareholder's manufacturing base. Debt at 60% of GDP in 2006 has risen to over 100% of GDP in the past 4-5 years and is now competing with debt ratios not seen since World War Two.

HEARN: "Gentlemen, I know each of you has been in discussion regarding solutions for these present day phenomenon. I think the revised summary statement, requires pause and reflection. Regarding our moving forward on solutions, I need to ensure we remind these shareholders of their decisions made in the past 30-40 years that eventually led them to this economic catastrophe. If we can link those decisions to the present day economic environment and communicate those to the shareholders, I feel 1776 LLC will be able to sustain the next 100 years or so. I need a plan that has immediate impact and grows the GDP from $15 Trillion to $25 Trillion in a short 5 year span. I want a plan that provides local impact with power moving from centralized governing bodies (federal) to decentralized government bodies (at the state level) and utilize the federal government in a way it was intended to be used in setting the playing field between the states and providing for the defense. And lastly, I want to educate the shareholders and provide a centralized governing body, at the private level, to communicate quarterly to the shareholders regarding these vital statistics in a way the average shareholder can understand them. We are now at war-an economic war to defend the liberties and freedoms granted by these shareholder's forefathers. Without a solid economic footing and without an ongoing mechanism to measure and communicate the country's performance, I fear our 1776 LLC experiment will erode.

"I recall the words of Thomas Jefferson '*I place economy among the first and most important virtues and public debt as the greatest of dangers to be feared. To preserve our independ-*

ence, we must not let our rulers load us with public debt. We must make our choice between economy and liberty or confusion and servitude. If we run into such debts, we must be taxed in our meat and drink, in our necessities and comforts, in our labor and in our amusements. If we can prevent the government from wasting the labor of the people, under the pretense of 'caring for them,' they will be happy.'"

HEARN: "It's been a long day gentlemen. Let us adjourn the meeting until tomorrow where we will get right into the specifics of turning this thing around-and turn it around quickly."

Chris Murtagh

CHAPTER 1

GROW AMERICA
49,551,703

"When people attempt to rebel against the iron logic of nature, they come into conflict with the very same principles to which they owe their existence as human beings, their actions against nature must lead to their own downfall."

—Adolph Hitler, Mein Kampf

Consumers drive the engine of the US economy. Our population, as of 2010, is 308,597,112 US citizens, driving an economic machine that consumes $14.9 trillion a year in goods and services. The USA gross domestic product of $14.2 trillion, less its exports of $1.8 trillion and then adding its imports of $2.5 trillion, shows a consumption of $14.9 trillion or about $48,283 per person. The USA workforce (those that actually are employed and working) measure approximately 150,000,000, or roughly 50 percent of the population. The rest of us are children, stay-at-home folks, unemployed, retirees, or others that typically depend upon these employed folks to keep the economy moving and pay for society's needs.

As unemployment varies, the power of the USA consumer is felt not only in the USA but around the world, as the USA consumer leads the world in goods purchased for each person.

Given these estimates of the power of each USA consumer at $48,283 per person, our focus is not on what the consumer is paying for but where the actual consumer is. It begs the question: If there were more US citizens purchasing goods and services at the levels outlined above, and these citizens drive the economic machine, wouldn't our economy be in a better position if there were more people buying stuff? In line with that thought process, it is not only consumers but the mix of consumers, what they buy, and how they spend that makes a great difference.

A younger married couple with four children will tend to spend a significant amount more than a married couple in their sixties. The younger couple buys homes, toys, clothes for school, cars, and extends their purchasing sometimes beyond their means, gambling that prosperity will eventually provide them a boost in income and increase their quality of life. The sixty-year-old couple isn't buying the toys, clothes, cars, or extending themselves to the same extent and is less willing to increase debt, as their goals are quite different. The driving force behind the economic machine is its population, earning abilities, mix of consumers, and desire to spend.

There have been 49,551,703 abortions in the USA since *Roe v. Wade* was introduced in 1973. The numbers were taken from the Internet from documented sources and relate to a potential in our population from 308,597,112 to well over 350,000,000 USA consumers if these aborted consumers were still here. These additional 50 million consumers, at $48,282 per consumer in 2009, would increase the spending by $2.4 trillion for the year 2009 alone.

If one considers the cumulative effect of these 50 million over time and considering the children that would have been born from these aborted persons (those aborted from 1973-1987 would be of adult age ranging from twenty-four to thirty-seven years old), the overall effect is nearly 70 million people that would be consuming products at the rate of $48,823 per person, or about $3.4 trillion in goods or services in 2009 alone. Assuming a 30 percent tax rate on these items consumed, the incremental alone would be $1.14 trillion in the government coffers. And that is only for the year 2009. On a worldwide basis, performed abortions to date are estimated at 1 billion or approximately 15 percent of the planet's current population. In the year 1800, the worldwide population was just less than the amount aborted over the past fifty years or so or approximately 980,000 million residents at that time.

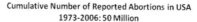

Cumulative Number of Reported Abortions in USA
1973-2006: 50 Million

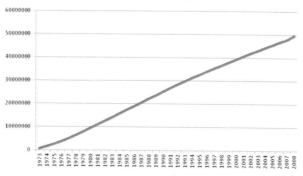

Watch out for this one: the cumulative loss from 1973-2011 is over $45.8 trillion in goods and serviced that would have been purchased by these aborted persons and lost tax revenues at 30 percent of $13.7 trillion from 1973-2011. The picture looking forward is grim, as we have only included the children of those aborted from 1973-1987. At that time the cumulative abortions (1973-1987) totaled only 20.1 million. The other 30 million happened during 1987-2009. We have not even begun the see the effects of this decision, as the children that would have been born from 1987-2009 would be another 30 million or so for a total effect of abortions plus the children that would have been born from those abortions near 100 million. And that assumes abortions only through 2009.

---

12   http://www.nrlc.org/abortion/facts/abortionstats.html

100 million persons are the size of California (37 million), Texas (24 million), New York (19 million), and Florida (18 million) combined.

The effect of this decision, purely from a consumption and taxable perspective, is compelling if we believe that the consumer is the driving factor that sustains the USA economy and that the increase or decrease in their consumption has dramatic effects on the economy as a whole.

We have only considered the purchasing power of these aborted persons and their unborn children. We have not considered the earnings power and tax revenues that would be collected from wages and payroll that would also add to our government coffers.

Figure number 12 summarizes a sobering consequence for the decision to remove these consumers as future contributors to the shareholders economic strength. The table lists the annual and cumulative effect with the estimate that only 70% of the APFW couples would bear 2 children each. The effect alone in 2011 shows approximately $3.1 Trillion in lost GDP or about 20% of 2011 estimated GDP of $15 Trillion. The impact makes sense as the affect of this decision summarizes to a loss of estimated 69 million due to the 1973 impact or 23% of today's total 310 million shareholders well within reasonable estimates.

More discouraging is the look ahead through 2035 given the 2011 activity plus 25 years total 120 million consumers contributing to a loss of GDP of $8.5 Trillion, with 2% annual growth, in 2035 due to this single shareholder decision.

Figure No: 12
Tax Potential: $13.7 Trillion Thru 2011 Affect of APFW and CTANH 1973-2035 (15)

Year	Number	APFW	25 Years	Couples (X.7)	CTANH	CUM CTANH	Total	GDP/Capita	Annual Loss
1973	744600	744600					744600	23244	$ 17,307,482,400
1974	898600	1643200					1643200	22901	$ 37,630,923,200
1975	1034200	2677400					2677400	22267	$ 59,617,665,800
1976	1179300	3856700					3856700	23611	$ 91,060,543,700
1977	1316700	5173400					5173400	24450	$ 126,489,630,000
1978	1409600	6583000					6583000	25542	$ 168,142,986,000
1979	1497700	8080700					8080700	26051	$ 210,510,315,700
1980	1553900	9634600					9634600	25675	$ 247,368,355,000
1981	1577300	11211900					11211900	26070	$ 292,294,233,000
1982	1573900	12785800					12785800	25321	$ 323,749,241,800
1983	1575000	14360800					14360800	26224	$ 376,597,619,200
1984	1577200	15938000					15938000	27866	$ 444,128,308,000
1985	1588600	17526600					17526600	28763	$ 504,117,595,800
1986	1574000	19100600					19100600	29486	$ 563,200,291,600
1987	1559100	20659700					20659700	30158	$ 623,055,232,600
1988	1590800	22250500					22250500	31114	$ 692,302,057,000
1989	1566900	23817400					23817400	31923	$ 760,322,860,200
1990	1608600	25426000					25426000	32157	$ 817,623,882,000
1991	1556500	26982500					26982500	31656	$ 854,158,020,000
1992	1528900	28511400					28511400	32279	$ 920,319,480,600
1993	1495000	30006400					30006400	32765	$ 983,159,696,000
1994	1423000	31429400					31429400	33684	$ 1,058,667,909,600
1995	1359400	32788800		260610	521220	521220	33310020	34122	$ 1,136,604,502,440
1996	1360200	34149000		314510	629020	1150240	35299240	34989	$ 1,235,085,108,360
1997	1335000	35484000		361970	723940	1874180	37358180	36112	$ 1,349,078,596,160
1998	1319000	36803000		412755	825510	2699690	39502690	37247	$ 1,471,356,694,430
1999	1314800	38117800		460845	921690	3621380	41739180	38599	$ 1,611,090,608,820
2000	1313000	39430800		493360	986720	4608100	44038900	39750	$ 1,750,546,275,000
2001	1291000	40721800		524195	1048390	5656490	46378290	39769	$ 1,844,418,215,010
2002	1269000	41990800		543865	1087730	6744220	48735020	40108	$ 1,954,664,182,160

2003	1250000	43240800		552055	1104110	7848330	51089130	41792	$ 2,135,116,920,960
2004	1222100	44462900		550865	1101730	8950060	53412960	42681	$ 2,279,718,545,760
2005	1206200	45669100		551250	1102500	10052560	55721660	43332	$ 2,414,530,971,120
2006	1242200	46911300		552020	1104040	11156600	58067900	43726	$ 2,539,076,995,400
2007	1209600	48120900		556010	1112020	12268620	60389520	43178	$ 2,607,498,694,560
2008	1212400	49333300		550900	1101800	13370420	62703720	41313	$ 2,590,478,784,360
2009	1200000	50533300		545685	1091370	14461790	64995090	42189	$ 2,742,077,852,010
2010	1200000	51733300		556780	1113560	15575350	67308650	43033	$ 2,896,478,327,547
2011	1200000	52933300		548415	1096830	16672180	69605480	43893	$ 3,055,223,653,787
2012	1200000	54133300		563010	1126020	17798200	71931500	44771	$ 3,220,467,076,119
2013	1200000	55333300		544775	1089550	18887750	74221050	45667	$ 3,389,432,680,224
2014	1200000	56533300		535115	1070230	19957980	76491280	46580	$ 3,562,968,794,808
2015	1200000	57733300		523250	1046500	21004480	78737780	47512	$ 3,740,963,129,061
2016	1200000	58933300		498050	996100	22000580	80933880	48462	$ 3,922,209,569,425
2017	1200000	60133300		475790	951580	22952160	83085460	49431	$ 4,107,008,807,905
2018	1200000	61333300		476070	952140	23904300	85237600	50420	$ 4,297,659,367,162
2019	1200000	62533300		467250	934500	24838800	87372100	51428	$ 4,493,385,952,602
2020	1200000	63733300		461650	923300	25762100	89495400	52457	$ 4,694,635,022,463
2021	1200000	64933300		460180	920360	26682460	91615760	53506	$ 4,901,979,393,530
2022	1200000	66133300		459550	919100	27601560	93734860	54576	$ 5,115,670,919,707
2023	1200000	67333300		451850	903700	28505260	95838560	55667	$ 5,335,092,035,836
2024	1200000	68533300		444150	888300	29393560	97926860	56781	$ 5,560,369,303,316
2025	1200000	69733300		437500	875000	30268560	100001860	57916	$ 5,791,753,335,815
2026	1200000	70933300		427735	855470	31124030	102057330	59075	$ 6,029,014,851,337
2027	1200000	72133300		422170	844340	31968370	104101670	60256	$ 6,272,779,473,739
2028	1200000	73333300		434770	869540	32837910	106171210	61461	$ 6,525,431,902,541
2029	1200000	74533300		423360	846720	33684630	108217930	62691	$ 6,784,250,716,422
2030	1200000	75733300		424340	848680	34533310	110266610	63944	$ 7,050,937,441,215
2031	1200000	76933300		420000	840000	35373310	112306610	65223	$ 7,325,011,796,153
2032	1200000	78133300		420000	840000	36213310	114346610	66528	$ 7,607,228,750,312
2033	1200000	79333300		420000	840000	37053310	116386610	67858	$ 7,897,804,377,919
2034	1200000	80533300		420000	840000	37893310	118426610	69216	$ 8,196,960,139,131
2035	1200000	81733300		420000	840000	38733310	120466610	70600	$ 8,504,923,009,039
2036	1200000	82933300		420000	840000	39573310	122506610	72012	$ 8,821,925,609,689

FUTURE

These CTANH (consumers that are not here) and APFW (aborted potential future workers) have a more complex twist, as the peak removal of these future contributors hit in 1990 at an annual rate of approximately 1,600,000 abortions in that year alone. Adding twenty-one years to that puts that peak in 2011. The decline in abortion rates show 2010 expected near 1,200,000 and holding steady. This decline may be attributed to over-the-counter medications that are effective in eliminating pregnancies, thus reducing the number of abortions. The cumulative effect, however, of these CTANH and APFW groups see the strength of their unearned powers in the years ahead.

OVERALL EFFECT

The economic impact of these groups is staggering. The consumption they offered and revenues from payroll and taxes that would have been paid are long gone. The future effect is also intimidating as the largest of all USA generations, the "baby boomers," already started retiring and will retire in record numbers over the next twenty years. The present rate of 1,200,000 abortions per year through 2035 would put the total impact of *Roe v. Wade* at over 120 million of these CTANH.

How does one compensate for these financial losses? Many will argue that the immigration efforts have offset these losses. Others would argue that immigration efforts should have been added to these losses and not simply offset. From a business perspective, we have downsized our families and citizens and have outsourced our manufacturing to overseas individuals. Unlike the early 1900s where immigration assisted in the eventual growth for USA, we were not at that time reducing the shareholder's future consumers to the same extent outlined in this chapter.

Now many will argue that if we had more of these consumers, we would be in a worse financial condition, unemployment would be even greater, and our nation would be in even worse shape. Perhaps given the road traveled and the programs put in place, many responding to this lack of consumer growth, perhaps the country would be in a worse position.

Business leaders, however, might argue that point since most would agree that it is always better to have more consumers buying things than less; and it is always better to be growing one's business than to watch it decline and drive up debt, as the country has done. Business leader would also argue that expansion through new developments and acquisitions have to be balanced with divesting businesses that are no longer in line with the company's growth strategies or are poorly performing business units that lack either effective management, or that another company can manage more effectively than it can.

1776, LLC EXECUTIVE MANAGEMENT TEAM MEETING

CEO- HEARN: "Ah come on, now!"

"What the heck are they doing to themselves?"

"They need these younger consumers, and they need to lower the average age disbursement back down to twenty-eight or thirty years of age. The average age for their work-force in 1978 was around thirty-five years old. In 2008 it was estimated at forty-one years old, and in twenty to thirty years, we may see this go to forty-nine to fifty years old as the average age in the workforce. Sixty-year-olds do not purchase toys, buy stereos, send their children to school, and buy start-up homes. They start to retire. Gentlemen, our markets are in decline, our debt has encumbered each of our net worth by $45,000 a share, and our existing consumer base has shrunk by over 50 million during the past thirty-seven years. We have been in business since 1776, and this recent impact since 1973 is quite substantial. We need to remedy this situation quickly, and I need to have a strategic direction soon to provide talking points for our shareholders

VP MANUFACTURING: YOUNG: "Our goal continues to be cost cutting and technology advancements to offset our decline in USA consumption by exporting our goods and services to Europe, Asia, the Middle East, and Africa. We cannot compete in the basic commodity manufactur-ing business effectively from a cost perspective with the

Chinese, the logistics of setting up manufacturing and distribution channels in Europe and Asia will require resources we do not have, and we are focusing now on shutting down obsolete plants in locations where we have lost business, and we have laid off the local workers. The unemployment is out of control hovering around 9-10% and their manufacturing plants are operating at around 75% capacity. If you add to that the number of unemployed out of work for over a year it's more likely in the range of 12%. We can't seem to get engineers and scientists that we need due to their declining math and science scores. Our energy costs are through the ceiling, and we cannot manufacture products competitively here in the USA. We just do not have the consumption. We are all screwed up. The federal and local governments are in the power and utility business and real estate markets; their postal service lost over $8.5 billion last year. They keep hanging on to outdated business models and keep piling up entitlement programs all over the place. The infrastructure we need to move goods and services are crumbling, oil and gas prices are causing skyrocketing costs for petrochemical products, our ability to move information quickly in medical information services is ridiculous, and we cannot seem to link where we should put the investments and where we should exit poorly performing businesses. So if we want a 5 year plan we need to address the China fair trade issues we discussed earlier and link the business development efforts to expansion of US manufacturing plants. I further suggest that growth plans are based upon those markets, especially manufacturing and construction, where local value added is considerable driving employment.

VP MARKETING: BRINSTER: "It's hell out there! Our declining USA consumer base, lack of spending on a world-wide basis, and global competition cutting costs make our commodity business weak. Our technology sector stays ahead of the curve, but lack of continued investments is not churning out new products as they should. We are in deep crap here, and I cannot cut the prices fast enough to stay afloat. Retail and restaurant industry is dying, office vacancies are near-record levels, new homes sales are dead--hell, we have 13 million vacant homes now--and we can't give them away.

At the end of the day, any single Chinese manufacturing facility can outperform our manufacturing processes due to their labor and material costs. This will continue to hamper our manufacturing growth on a worldwide basis. We have lost the clothing industry, plastics, steel and iron, and any high commodity non-differentiated products to the Chinese. India is increasing its share of technology and manufacturing support, and it's simply a matter of time when these less developed nations will provide worldwide leadership. Let's face it, gentlemen, it is what it is. In addition, we keep taxing our base and adding employees to the government administration areas.

We do, however, have a sustainable competitive advantage in our consumers and in our freedom and liberty as I mentioned in our opening discussions. Let's face it, we need more consumers. I came up with a plan to increase our market share of the worldwide consumer. Right now we have 4.4% percent of the world's population living in the USA. We will increase that to 5.5 percent by importing the consumers and increasing our immigration like we did back in the early 1900s. By taking the competition's consumers, we increase market share and spending in the USA. Please refer to my first slide regarding 80 Million new Citizens or what we in marketing call the "Grow America Campaign"

Profile of New Citizens: Target 80 Million Grow America Campaign

---

- 13 Million Families, each with four children and married parents.
- Earning power at 1.5-2.0 times USA average (today at $40,000)
- Pass a proficiency and IQ test to ensure competency
- No criminal records
- 20 percent will come from Asia (16 Million)
- 20 percent will come from Europe (16 Million)
- 15 percent will come from Mexico (12 Million)
- 10 percent will come from Africa (8 Million)
- 10 percent will come from India (8 Million)
- 10 percent will come from the Middle East (8 Million)
- The balance from Russia and Eastern Europe

"By absorbing more share of the world's population and customer base, and importing these consumers to the USA quickly, the impact is quite significant for local consumption of goods and services and will set the stage for increasing tax revenues quickly."

VP HUMAN RESOURCES: BLACKWELL: "That equates to 16 million per year over the next five years, or a rate of 1,300,000 per month. At six per household (two parents and four children), that will require 13 million homes. That is an undertaking of enormous proportions. It would tax our school systems and require tremendous construction for support facilities; our manufacturing facilities could not keep up with the immediate demand, and we would have to change our internal processes and hire an immense amount of people to make this happen. On the other hand, we have around 13 million vacant homes. If we could devise a program to absorb these vacant homes with the new shareholders, it would spark tremendous development, drive the housing industry and increase GDP by $48,238 per head, or $4 trillion, and would raise GDP from $15 trillion to $19 trillion.

VP FINANCE: DARBON: "Guys we are in deep crap here! Debt is increasing, revenues have fallen, consumers are not borrowing, and banks are not lending. If these 80 million have liquidly of $100,000 from each family household (13 million new family households), new consumer imported, that would immediately put $1.3 trillion onto our bank savings and checking accounts. I would add that as a factor when considering the profile.

"We would also need 26 million new cars (two per household) per year over the next five years, about 5 million per year, which or about 50 percent greater than 2010 USA consumption). At $30,000 per car, the revenues to the auto industry would be $150 billion per year over the next five years, or almost $1 trillion. The auto industry would have to increase employment and size quickly. At $7500 per person *per year* in healthcare, that would increase the health care revenues by $600 billion to the health care industry in five years. I can go on and on."

"Staying in tune with this discussion, the profile of these new residents would have to also include certain professions, and I would like to modify that profile as follows: Each family has liquidity of $100,000 to be deposited in USA banks. In line with marketing's concept to import 80 Million new residents in the next 7 years, I prepared a slide to further define those new shareholders and provide the following overview:

> ## Profile of New Citizens: Target 80 Million Grow America Campaign
>
> ---
>
> - 10 percent medical background
> - 10 percent engineering/science
> - 10 percent teachers
> - 10 percent manufacturing background
> - 10 percent power and utility background
> - 10 percent construction industry background
> - 10 percent agricultural background
> - 10 percent banking and finance
> - 10 percent government liaison related by country
> - 10 percent other as required

VP BUSINESS DEVELOPMENT: GETHER: "I'll take that a step further! We design an incentive business development plan supporting the Grow America Campaign expediting the process and absorbing the existing inventories of vacant homes. I prepared an overview for the group's consideration:

> ### Profile of New Citizens: Target 80 Million Grow America Campaign
>
> 1. Import 80 million of the selected criteria of new consumers in five years.
>
> 2. We provide to these new consumers a free home and locate them in one of the vacant thirteen million homes in the USA.
>
> 3. We provide to each of these consumers two electric/gas-driven General Motors Volt or equivalent cars free of charge in their garages.
>
> 4. We allocate these new consumers to each state based upon local state needs.
>
> 5. We require them to stay put for five years and give them the option to purchase the home at 15 percent off market levels in five years. They pay all local taxes, utilities, and living expenses.
>
> 6. They own the car after year five."

VP FINANCE DARBON: "I like the growth plan but who is going to pay for that? We are going broke now!"

VP BUSINESS DEVELOPMENT" GETHER: "We are going to divest the government interests in real estate and sell those to private investors who can better manage it, we are going to divest the government from utilities and sell those to utility companies, and we are going to divest several other nonperforming businesses. My plan is to raise $4-5 trillion from existing businesses the government should not be in and put those funds to use in growth-related industries. Let's just say I found the money and we need to create a budget to support this initiative.

"It's incredible the amount of equity and value tied up in these government businesses that serve little or no purpose in defending the nation or providing for the welfare of the shareholders. Hey, it's the shareholders' money and the shareholders' future at stake here."

"My guys have been working on this for some time. I'll give you the overview at the end of this first session."

VP RESEARCH AND DEVELOPMENT: THORPE: "I like what I am hearing. This plan does not require leading technological advancements and can have a significant impact on the economy. I would recommend, however, that we consider natural gas driven vehicles since the USA has 100 year supply of natural gas available and brings with it about a 40-45% reduction in greenhouse gas emissions as compared to coal fired power plants that provide electricity to those 26 Million cars you mentioned above.

VP BUSINESS DEVELOPMENT: GETHER: "Good point, Sam. The natural gas infrastructure is not in place now at the gas pumps and will take years before these guys pipe the gas to those gas stations. They have the product and are working on its transmission and eventual distribution at the retail levels. I suggest that is a different phase and not in the first 5-7 years as John requested. Agreed?"

THORPE: "Given the short term plan, I agree"

VP BUSINESS DEVELOPMENT: GETHER: "Table No: 3 outlines the initiative and costs associated with its execution. Table No: 4 outlines the effect on tax revenues from expected growth in salaries from these initiatives.

Table No: 3 Grow America Campaign Budget

Initiative	Objective	Required Processing	Budget (ea)	Total Annual Budget
Immigration Office	2.7 Million Households per year	5000 processors	$80,000	$0.4 Billion
Home Processing	2.7 Million Homes per year	5000 processors	$80,000	$0.4 Billion
Electric Cars	5.4 Million per year		$30,000	$162 Billion
Purchase Homes	2.7 Million per year		$75,000	$202 Billion
Home Purchase	5 years after		($75,000)	($202 Billion)
Sub-Total				$162.8 Billion
Contingency			10%	$17 Billion
Annual				$180 Billion
5 Year Budget				**$900 Billion**

Table No: 4 Grow America Campaign Returns

Initiative	Objective	Numbers	Salary/Impact	Tax revenues: 30%
Employment	$160,000 per year-per HH-2 workers	13 Million HH	$2.0 Trillion	$624 Billion
GDP Absorption	$48,000 per resident-GDP Incremental	80 Million	$3.8 Trillion	$1.14 Trillion
Auto Car Revenues	$30,000 per car	13 Million	$0.4 Trillion	$0.012 Trillion
Auto Workers-Added	$100,000 per worker (all in)	1 Million	$0.1 Trillion	$0.03 Trillion
Indirect Workers-3X	$75,000 per worker (all in)	3 Million	$0.2 Trillion	$0.06 Trillion
Processors salaries			$0.08 Trillion	$0.02
Total			**$8.8 Trillion**	**$2.66 Trillion**

DARBON: "What about the costs for new manufacturing expansion plants, construction employment associated with those expansions, new schools, hospitals and other infrastructure costs? There are considerable tax revenues and costs associated with these. Who will execute this plan?"

GETHER: "The states. Each state has incentives associated with capturing these tax revenues and reducing unemployment in their areas, at the local basis. I suggest we have the States and not the Fed drive the allocation process. Let the Fed do what it is supposed to do by processing these new citizens quickly and by arranging the ground rules. Let the banks loose on funding the expansion through local bonds and loans based upon this explosive growth. The States will find a way to finance their infrastructure growth as we increase the US population 25% in the next 5 years. The early budget only starts the ball rolling. As I mentioned earlier, we found over $4 Trillion in liquidity by altering the Fed's present day business model that we can use for short term loans or guarantees to the States to plug the gap, but I will get into those details later.

BLACKWELL: 5,000 processors mean that each processor is moving 45 families per month or 11 per week. That's a significant effort. That may require software and hardware and other investments. I noticed you included $17 Billion for contingency and that might work.

GETHER: "The effect does not take into consideration that the 13 Million vacant homes are now off the market. The impact for new housing and construction will go from zero to 100 miles per hour with significant impacts to local and federal revenues–and a long way from where it is today. The plan fixes the housing market and drives future new home construction."

HEARN: "I like the thought process. We need to replace these CTANH and APFW's that were lost from the mid-1970 through today. This new mix should also reduce the average workers age and increase GDP consumption per capita given a shift in lower age and related consumption. I would also encourage as a part of the "Grow America Campaign" that we attempt to push the birthrate up to 3.5 per household that will take us further down the growth path after 2050 or so. This initiative alone should bring the unemployment rate down to about 7% or so when completed in its fifth year. If we include the construction of new manufacturing facilities and associated infrastructure costs to support this growth, it may drop to 6%. Have your guys look at that and lets have the plan ready in the next month so we can review this with the 50 state governors and hash out the allocations of these new citizens. This additional $3.8 Trillion in GDP when added to the existing $15 Trillion gets us to about $18.5 Trillion. Good job guys."

It may sound funny and to some insulting, but keep in mind, this is not a political overview but one of the numbers. Acquiring new consumers is done every day as businesses acquire companies and look to distribute their products and services to this new pool of consumers.

America was built on rapid expansion into new territories with innovative growth strategies including the Land Rush of 1890's along with immigration policies in the early 1900's, all supporting growth and expansion. For the first twenty-five years of a person's life, they expand, grow, educate, move, marry, and plan for change. In our last twenty-five years of life, we plan for minor if any changes, risk little, and stay put, shrink, and then die.

The USA grew both in population and territory from 1776 up to the land acquisition in Alaska in 1867 and Hawaii annexation in 1898. The territory expansion from the thirteen colonies to the vast expansion of the USA's fifty states took less than 100 years. Since 1860 our rate of growth has been in decline. If this was a business, the shareholders would be "up in arms."

The impact of removing (aborting) 50 million consumers over a thirty-seven-year period with the compound effect forecast ahead to 2030 of 120 million simply gone has and will have a continued effect on the coffers in the USA. Did we do the right thing? The numbers are awesome. The shareholders decided on reducing its consumer base and are perhaps paying the price of that now.

CHAPTER 2

WEED-OUT AMERICA
$118,000,000,000

Prohibition will work great injury to the cause of temperance. It is a species of intemperance within itself, for it goes beyond the bounds of reason in that it attempts to control a man's appetite by legislation, and makes a crime out of things that are not crimes. A prohibition law strikes a blow at the very principles upon which our government was founded.

—Abraham Lincoln

According to the study, "Lost Taxes and Other Costs of Marijuana Laws," reported by *Forbes* (1 October 2007), marijuana consumption in the USA is around $118 billion per year business, considering the USA consumes 33 million pounds at approximately $3570/lb. at retail prices. With a taxable rate at around 30 percent, the government is missing out on approximately $35 billion a year in tax revenues.

According to the International Narcotics Control Strategy Report (INCSR), of the 15,000 metric tons of marijuana harvested (or about 33 million pounds), 10,000 metric tons are grown in the USA and 5,000 metric tons are imported from Mexico, South America, and other places. The agency estimates the pot is consumed by around 20 million "stoners" each year.

Retail prices, provided by the *Marijuana Prices Directory,* vary depending on where you live in the USA and the quality of what is being sold. According to the pricing quotes and quality of product sold, pricing varies from $2600 to $5000 per pound of reefer. We have settled on $3570/lb or around $2.50 for a "joint" or 1500 joints per pound.

The question of legalizing a recreational drug, like marijuana, has been a topic of immense debate. On one hand, we allow the consumption of tobacco in pipe, cigar, chewing, and cigarette form, we allow the consumption of alcohol in all conceivable forms, and we allow the consumption of controlled drugs in way too many forms.

Marijuana, however, teases us and tugs at our common sense far too often. Most believe that it is only a matter of time, maturity, and a changing culture that will eventually lead to its legalization. The steps from "reefer madness" to our present society have been baby steps at best.

The cost, however, for this decision and its continued delays in eventually making marijuana legal have been awesome in their scale.

The *Forbes* story outlines marijuana accounts for approximately 5 percent of arrests in the United States, costing the taxpayers $10 billion a year. If it were grown in the USA, it would impair the drug cartels of Mexico and South America, employ directly and indirectly millions of US citizens, and improve the agricultural industry. Its legalization would most likely increase its consumption threefold from 20 million to 60 million consumers, providing an industry of $339 billion with annual tax revenues of $85 billion.

RATE OF ILLEGAL MARIJUANA TRANSACTIONS

According to table 13, violent crime arrests have declined about 18 percent over the past thirty years and property crime arrests have declined approximately 22 percent in the same period. Marijuana has bucked the system. Arrests related to marijuana have increased 114 per cent from 401,982 in 1980 to 858,408 in 2009.

Figure No: 13 USA Arrests: 1980-2009 By Category[13]

				US Arrests			
Year	Total Arrests	Total Drug Arrests	Total Marijuana Arrests	Marijuana Trafficking/Sale Arrests	Marijuana Possession Arrests	Total Violent Crime Arrests	Total Property Crime Arrests
2009	13,687,241	1,663,582	858,408	99,815	758,593	581,765	1,728,285
2008	14,005,615	1,702,537	847,863	93,640	754,224	594,911	1,687,345
2007	14,209,365	1,841,182	872,720	97,583	775,137	597,447	1,610,088
2006	14,380,370	1,889,810	829,627	90,711	738,916	611,523	1,540,297
2005	14,094,186	1,846,351	786,545	90,471	696,074	603,503	1,609,327
2004	13,938,071	1,746,570	773,731	87,329	686,402	586,558	1,644,197
2003	13,639,479	1,678,192	755,186	92,300	662,886	597,026	1,605,127
2002	13,741,438	1,538,813	697,082	83,096	613,986	620,510	1,613,954
2001	13,699,254	1,586,902	723,628	82,519	641,109	627,132	1,618,465
2000	13,980,297	1,579,566	734,497	88,455	646,042	625,132	1,620,928
1999	14,355,600	1,557,100	716,266	85,641	630,626	644,770	1,676,100
1998	14,528,300	1,559,100	682,885	84,191	598,694	675,900	1,805,600
1997	15,284,300	1,583,600	695,201	88,682	606,519	717,750	2,015,600
1996	15,168,100	1,506,200	641,642	94,891	546,751	729,900	2,045,600
1995	15,119,800	1,476,100	588,964	85,614	503,350	796,250	2,128,600
1990	14,195,100	1,089,500	326,850	66,460	260,390	705,500	2,217,800
1980	10,441,000	580,900	401,982	63,318	338,664		

Estimated annual law enforcement and prevention costs of $10 Billion a year, and climbing, do not appear to have curtailed its use. When expenses rise, over a 30 year period with those expenses designed to curtail an activity, and the activity increases by 114% over a thirty year period, the

13   Crime in the United States 2009," FBI Uniform Crime Report (Washington, DC: US Dept. of Justice, September 2010), Table 29, http://www2.fbi.gov/ucr/cius2009/data/table_29.html and Arrest Table: Arrests for Drug Abuse Violations, http://www2.fbi.gov/ucr/cius2009/arrests/index.html.

Chris Murtagh

experiment should be scrapped. Many would argue that the rate of increase would be greater if these costs were not expended. Others would argue that the shareholders, poor devils, are too ignorant to make these decisions on their own and that higher levels of governing authorities will be required to limit individual freedoms because they simply know better.

THE NEW BUSINESS

The growing, processing, distribution, and retail outlets would employ millions of people. The distribution centers, retail outlets, and warehouses moving 99 million pounds of marijuana, assuming consumption would triple if legalized; a year is an interesting thought. Assuming a 1500 square foot retail outlet would sell $4 million of marijuana per year, the need would require 85,000 retail outlets, each paying $16 per square foot, or annual lease payments of $2 billion per year to anxious retail landlords and require a combined 128 million square feet of leased retail space to support sales.

A conservative income multiplier, or the effect of $339 billion in new legal revenues, is estimated at two times the revenues for this newly introduced product where the new dollars find their way into salaries, new homes, new car purchases and other areas of economic grow. For every $339 billion spent purchasing the golden weed, the conservative effect is two-fold or $678 billion in all, for total tax revenues of $170 billion and employ additional two million people-indirectly. The assets required to provide for these revenues are estimated at approximately 50% of revenues or $339 Billion in property, plants and equipment to produce the end product.

What would be the economic effects of legalizing marijuana?

- Create $678 billion annual revenues direct and indirect.
- Tax revenues of $170 billion.
- Increase in direct employment of 1 million people.
- Cause for increase in indirect employment of 2 million people.
- Improve quality and distribution of the product.
- Lower crime rates and arrests by over 800,000 per year at an estimated arrest and processing cost of $10 billion.
- Lower dependence on foreign countries.
- Lower taxes on the American consumer.
- Raise GDP by $678 Billion

From a historical perspective, can we learn from lessons in the past regarding this decision to keep marijuana illegal? Hum—let's see. Is there any other product or service, from our historical past, that was viewed as immoral, made its consumers inebriated, was sold on the black market, was associated with violence and gangs, and was successfully kept off the market?

PROHIBITION:
A HISTORICAL OVERVIEW

Prohibition lasted from January 16, 1920, to December 15, 1933. It created a booming illegal industry, drove up crime rates, and was generally accepted as one of the worst laws ever enacted on the US society. Homicide rates increased 78 percent from pre-Prohibition (prior to 1920) rates of 5.4 per 100,000 to 10 per 100,000 at its peak in 1933. After Prohibition was repealed, homicide rates dropped back to 5.0 per 100,000 by 1944. By 1932 the number of federal convicts increased 561 percent, with two-thirds of all prisoners convicted of alcohol and drug-related charges. Organized crime, however, got its strong roots during Prohibition, with over thirteen years from 1920-1933 to define its charter, organize its processes, and provide the goods and services to the American people.

As organized crime got its big boost and start during these times, it eventually led to this business unit expanding in the gambling industry and into prostitution and drugs (along with a list of other industries and services). Organized crime was successful because it gave the consumer what it wanted and when it needed it. It had a high regard for its business and services and controlled their process through highly organized management systems. Quality of services, customer satisfaction, and its need to grow and expand allowed this business unit to flourish. Did Prohibition provide the need? Did Prohibition provide the initial cash flow to allow organized crime to flourish?

As big business took over the gambling industry in Las Vegas and state regulators allowed the expansion into other states, revenues left the organized crime business and went into the coffers of the shareholders. Legalized liquor sales following Prohibition also depleted the revenues for organized crime. The eventual crackdown on organized crime shifted the distribution of illegal drugs from the US shores to other countries. The fact that the USA is the largest consumer of illegal drugs is not disputed. The business model, however, of shifting revenues from organized crime figures in the USA to international markets hurt the spending of these organized crime figures and put the money in overseas drug cartels that spend the money outside the USA. Again the discussion is not about the moral dilemma of drugs and their use. It is about the numbers.

Time after time with liquor, gambling, or other vices, the American consumer will get what it desires. Perhaps it's the notion that freedom allows us to make our own decisions that affect us personally. Critics would argue that liquor, gambling, and other vices hurt communities. Overeating eventually leads to health problems that we all pay for. While the argument is effective on both sides, once the venting and personal opinions of Americans are put aside, the fact that the USA is the leading consumer of illegal drugs is still there. The USA is gaining weight every day through overeating. Smoking, while declining, has done so not necessarily due to free choice, as it is from increased taxing, increased isolation, and increased consumer education on its eventual health concerns.

According to the CATO Institute's February 6th, 2003, report, government intervention in New York to increase cigarette tax only assisted in strengthening black market profiteers.

Thanks to recent city and state level tax hikes, New York City now has the highest cigarette taxes in the country—a combined state and local tax rate of $3.00 per pack. Consumers have responded by turning to the city's bustling black market and other low-tax sources of cigarettes. During the four months following the recent tax hikes, sales of taxed cigarettes in the city fell by more than 50 percent compared to the same period the prior year.

California, as it always does, leads the nation in this change. California is awesome in its ability to set these trends. Perhaps it is California's belief that its people make the decisions, perhaps it is in its belief that the government's job is to listen to its voters, but whatever it does from legalizing marijuana to gay marriage to funding illegal immigrants and providing them with licenses, and California has led the revolution of change since the 1960s.

Mendocino County in northern California generates approximately $1 billion from its "Emerald Triangle," providing tax revenues of approximately $250 million on those legal sales. Yes, the federal and state governments actually get tax revenues from legalized sales of marijuana. That means the drug cartels need to make up that $1 billion in sales. Sounds almost like the Prohibition days where the government (the people) took a common sense approach. While California is still struggling with the laws of growing, distributing, and other regulations, there will, no doubt, be increases in theft crime and other human interactions driven by greed in the shorter term. Eventually California will regulate this industry as it has with other legal and viable industries and bring order to that chaos. I would expect California will eventually produce and sell $10 billion of marijuana within the next five to ten years and lessen its dependence for this drug from overseas cartels. They regulated mining during the gold and silver rush days of the 1800 and will no doubt regulate this new "weed" rush (there's a play on words) in our modern days. Look to California to set the new pace of common sense by the numbers. Where is the Come-On! Cents perspective with regards to regulating marijuana?

1776 LLC EXECUTIVE MANAGEMENT TEAM

CEO: HEARN: "Okay, we have a new cash crop that has been cleared for consumption in California. It's risky because the state law makes it legal, but the federal law still considers it illegal. There are consumption issues, distribution issues, and legal business-related issues, but it appears Mendocino County is on the forefront of something new. The market is sized at approximately $390 billion once approved across the USA, considering current consumption will go from $130 billion to $390. How do we get our hands around this? We have been in business since 1776. How the heck did we allow this crop to go offshore and not get the revenues from it?"

VP MANUFACTURING: YOUNG: "In order to actually manufacture this crop, I turned to the guys in the agricultural department to provide some insight. We would need to follow existing state and federal guidelines for water consumption, water treatment, and chemical treatment and could grow the crops in the Sunbelt states in a very effective manner. We would need to grow in a controlled environment and build greenhouses. Our designs call for solar-powered greenhouses that would reduce energy consumption and lower costs of production.

"Assuming we got 100 percent market share and could shut down the cartels in Mexico and South America, we would need to produce 99million pounds of the stuff, assuming consumption is forecast to be three times existing consumption.

"We would require about five thousand 100,000-square-foot greenhouses, with each greenhouse harvesting 18,200 pounds per year. Each would employ fifty people for a total of 250,000 employees. We need eighty-five thousand 1500-square-foot retail outlets, each employing five people for a total of 425,000 folks. Our trucking services shipping from the greenhouses would require about 5,000 additional trucks at a cost of around $500 million. The sales, marketing, and R&D groups require additional 150,000 for the testing of new products and marketing and distribution sales efforts. Our finance and collection require additional 35,000 people for financing and collections, and our IT, and production services group needs about 75,000 for new software development and ongoing support. Overhead, management and real estate coordination would employ about 50,000. Quality control testing and reporting are about another 10,000. At the end of the day, we are looking at approximately 1 million employees associated directly with this new crop and an indirect effect of two times that for a total of 3 million direct and indirect employees."

VP MARKETING: BRINSTER: "It's about time! The importers have controlled this market for years. South America has been one of the largest recipients of these untaxed revenues, and we could not even compete. We can have the stores leased out in about six to ten months, hire the workforce and train them in about the same time, and will be ready for sales and local customer support in as short a timeframe. Man, we have been waiting for this decision for some time."

"We are going to reinvent this market. We will have online order processing systems, distribution channels with 85,000 outlets, flavored enhanced joints, providing consumers with endless choices, strong TV advertising, and elevated quality control systems in place to ensure high product quality and delivery. Prices will stay the same at $3570/pound, and the consumers will beat a path to the door. Our takeout services will package the product in cartons or individual packs for the consumer's enjoyment. We will need to talk to the legal guys about making consumption available only from FDA-approved growing facilities and limit imports, but I'm sure we can get that done. We are ready to go, have product samples, and need about *twenty four* months to 'roll out' (no pun intended) this new product. I'd also like to explore the export market and ensure we have the highest quality product with exceptional marketing and promotional efforts. The challenge is deriving a retail pricing structure for this product and understanding the consumer. We haven't factored in the 80 million new consumers into the equation, and we are considering only 60 million consumers.

"I'd prefer not to give this product to the liquor, beer, and wine manufacturers. They understand how to market inebriation-type products to consumers and have a channel to that market already established. I would also exclude the tobacco guys, as they serve a different *product and* market segment. We need out-of-the-box thinking and market channels. We call this one "Weed-Out America."

VP FINANCE DARBON: "I like the concept! Everything is local to the USA: a higher level of employment, increase in agricultural market revenues, higher controlled quality, and drop in prison rates. You guys can 'roll out' a $390 billion new cash crop, providing tax revenues of $98 billion, and do it in less than the five-year period? Wow, why the hell have we been waiting so long on this? In addition, we get to save approximately $10 billion in prison-related costs. I like this more and more."

VP BUSINESS DEVELOPMENT: GETHER: "There are over 14 million unemployed people. We need engineers, contractors, marketing guys, and salespeople. Office and retail centers have vacancy rates of 15-20 percent, and we can have those under contract in a short period of time. We need agricultural experts to ensure we have the highest quality product with the most outstanding distribution system in the world. The shareholder's have some of the leading agricultural sciences and support staff along with some of the best farmland in the world." Once legalized and regulated, I feel the export market would have the potential to double sales for the US and double the employment opportunity."

VP HUMAN RESOURCES: BLACKWELL: "The American spirit was based upon certain freedoms of choice where I feel marijuana has proven itself as an acceptable recreational drug of choice. I don't drink or smoke but I would defend anyone's right to do so. In saying that, I appreciate that we are not discussing heroin, cocaine or other recreational drugs that, hypocritically, I am opposed to given today's environment. I am not looking to inebriate the shareholders but it is their choice, not mine. Once the government bodies enter the arena and attempt to control the shareholder's choice of food, clothing, recreational drug or any other freedom and are not consistent in that approach, black market forces come into play. I think we learned our lesson with regards to Prohibition, the only amendment that was ever reversed in the history of the country."

CEO: HEARN: "The shareholders have mixed feelings about this, and many only see the negative side. The trend, however, appears to be shifting to longer term acceptance. They all know it will be legal someday, and they all know that that no one is winning any war against drugs. I too have mixed feelings, but our primary role here is not to use our own sense of judgment but to allow the shareholders to develop this great society in the way they wish to do so. Jeff, have you and the guys worked out a basic budget?"

VP FINANCE: DARBON: "The marketing guys feel we can reach 100% of the forecast USA market share by year 7 given the black market infrastructure that would eventually be peeled back. During the first 7 years overall cumulative sales of $1.2 Trillion would reap tax revenues at 30% for around $129 Billion. After year 7, annual sales of $400 Billion would provide tax revenues of $38 Billion per year. I summarized this in Table No: 5"

Table No: 5 Marijuana Sales forecast: Year 1-7 ($ Billions)

Item	Year 1	Year 2	Year 3	Year 4	Year 5	Year 6	Year 7
Market Size	$130	$175	$220	$285	$325	$390	$400
Revenues	$20	$50	$75	$125	$250	$325	$400
Market Share	15%	29%	34%	44%	77%	60%	100%
COGS	$10	$25	$38	$63	$125	$163	$200
Gross Profit$	$10	$25	$37	$62	$125	$162	$200
SG&A	$4	$9	$13	$23	$45	$59	$72
Income	$6	$16	$24	$39	$80	$103	$128
30% Tax	$1.8	$4.8	$7.2	$12	$24	$31	$38
Employment-Direct	67,000	168,000	252,000	420,000	840,000	1,092,000	1,344,000
Employment-Indirect	67,000	168.000	252,000	420,000	840,000	1,092000	1,344,000
Total Employment	134,000	336,000	504,000	840,000	1,680,000	2,184,000	2,688,000

"The initiative would employ an estimated 3 Million over the period reducing unemployment from around 7% (following the Grow America Plan) to about 5% with this initiative. In addition, we feel the reduction in prison and associated costs estimated at around $10 Billion per year would save tax payers $70 Billion over the seven year term for the following total contribution:

Table No: 6 Contribution of "Weed –Out America"

Item	7 Year Outlook	Investment
Tax revenues		
Business	$129 Billion	Private
Payroll	$250 Billion	Private
Cost Savings		
Prisons	$70 Billion	Private
Unemployment	$3 Billion	Private
Total Return	**$452 Billion**	

Chris Murtagh

DARBON: "We see no investments required by the government for this program outside their normal regulatory processes. Private industry would provide the capital and investments. All we need to do is to move the government out of the way and let the shareholders decide if they want this product and service and vote accordingly."

HEARN: "Just move out of the way, give the people what they want and stop with this game of controlling shareholder's desires. I wonder if the support services group (especially the government services) really understands the principles of free choice. Ok, get the boys together on this one as well."

According to a number of independent sources–one including–Hemp: Lifeline to the Future, by Chris Conrad, 1994, pp. 192-193, part of Chapter 16, "A World of Cannabis Cultures." Did the Founding Fathers of the United States of America smoke cannabis? Some researchers think so. Dr. Burke, president of the American Historical Reference Society and a consultant for the Smithsonian Institute, counted seven early presidents as cannabis smokers: George Washington, Thomas Jefferson, James Madison, James Monroe, Andrew Jackson, Zachary Taylor and Franklin Pierce. "Early letters from our founding fathers refer to the pleasures of hemp smoking," said Burke. Pierce, Taylor and Jackson, all military men, smoked it with their troops. Cannabis was twice as popular among American soldiers in the Mexican

War as in Vietnam: Pierce wrote to his family that it was "about the only good thing" about that war.

I agree its "reaching" and subject to debate. But "come-on cents" forces us to look at this business of manufacturing and consuming marijuana and understand the opportunity left behind, costs associated with crime prevention programs that did not work during the Prohibition days and are not working now and the impact legalization would have in crippling the drug cartels. The question of one's moral thinking will certainly be challenged, as it should be. The question of those in the society who wish to control any substance consumed by their fellow shareholder that may do its society harm, need to be weighed against personal freedoms and liberties of each of the shareholders and not those who simply know better. The larger question of individual freedom is at stake. From a common sense approach we all understand the negative effects of smoking which is mentioned as the leading cause of death in the USA–yet smoking is legal, overweight Americans and propensity for diabetes from eating poorly selected diets are at record levels–yet we only suggest which foods are better than others–instead of making ice cream or hamburgers illegal, excessive alcohol consumption causes liver failure and the list goes on and on–yet these are all legal. Adding to these liberties is recent increase in the sales and distribution of legal drugs and the effect that action has on the shareholder's physical condition. If these were all judged illegal tomorrow, the prisons would overflow and there would be riots in the streets. Why? What is it about the America consumer's liberties and freedom that make this controversial topic more than simply entertaining?

Chris Murtagh

While I am not suggesting the Declaration of Independence or the Monroe Doctrine was drafted when the authors were stoned, and am not suggesting that marijuana will all of a sudden provide enlightenment to the masses, I do propose it is a matter of free choice and will continue to fuel an untaxed and unregulated industry that, by all accounts, will continue to grow in popularity. Come on now, you can purchase cigarettes, pipe tobacco, whisky, and all kinds of foods that lead to an overweight nation and eventual diabetes; but hands off the marijuana? I think we all know that, in time, this recreational drug will eventually be legalized and eventually put an end to the wasted drug prevention programs, loss of tax dollars, loss of employment opportunity and increased freedoms. If what Dr. Burke suggests; that the founding fathers smoked pot is true, then if you are not chucking by now or at least cracked a smile you must be "Bogartting that joint"..And no, I don't partake in the weed or drink. But frankly, after considering this chapter...I wish I did!

CHAPTER 3

OPERATION CELL SOLDIER
$100,000,000,000

"The efficiency of our criminal justice system is only barred by the difficulty of finding twelve men every day who don't know anything and can't read."

—Mark Twain

The USA spends $100 billion a year for its police ($30 billion), corrections ($25 billion) and judicial ($45 billion), housing only 2.4 million prisoners with an additional 5.1 Million on probation or parole. Overall judicial system expenditures are estimated at $200 billion a year.

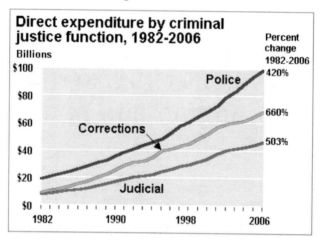

The total number of those in the "corrections mode" is approximately 7.5 million people.

In 1980 there were approximately 500,000 people in state, federal, and local prisons. That amount has more than quadrupled to 2,400,000 in 2008. Many were repeat offenders.

Of that population, approximately 1.5 million are in state and federal prisons; 800,000 are in local jails; and 100,000 are in juvenile facilities, with the balance in smaller jail facilities. In addition, there are almost 8 million previous inmates on probation.

A 2002 study showed that of approximately 275,000 inmates released in 1994, 67.5 percent were rearrested

---

14   U.S. Bureau of Justice Statistics.

Chris Murtagh

within three years of release, and 52 percent were back in prison. Direct expenditures of correctional officers from 1982 to 2006 grew 660 percent over that period, growing from $10 billion in 1982 to $65 million in 2006.

It is estimated that it costs the government approximately $20,000 per inmate per year, or $48 billion per year, to house these individuals. Productivity gains for society, revenues from employment, and even absorption of goods and services are all lost in this expenditure.

These are "sunk costs" that go to individuals that do not purchase any goods or services and do not contribute back to society's business model. Given that these inmates have quadrupled since 1980 and given that expenses are over $30 billion, the "come-on" cents approach is to look into this cornucopia of opportunity and test the ongoing business model.

Figure No: 18

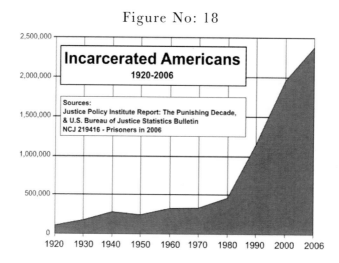

If the trend continues, by 2030 the population in prisons would exceed 6.4 million at an annual expense of $128 billion.

Remember the exercise is to point out our decisions, their consequences, and the economic effect. The trend in prison population, costs, and forecasts require pause and review.

These incarcerated persons broke the law and are required to pay their debt to society. However, society foots the bill of $65-plus billion per year. What debt is being paid back?

Defending the public that the criminals once dishonored may be a solution.

Insanity has many definitions. One in particular comes to mind: "If you continue doing what you are doing, and there is no change and you expect a change," one may define that as insanity. However, if you are doing what you are doing and the rates of expenditures increases by 660 percent, and the rate of failure is multiplied by five times over the same term that is not insanity. That is suicide!

We all know this exists. We may not have known the numbers until we read this book, but the issue of crime, prison rapes, and poor success rates-given the revolving door data- within our prisons is an ongoing area of focus and should give us pause. Regardless of the argument and regardless of your point of view, this thing is broken and needs to be fixed. But where is our "come-on" cents?

In 2006, there were 1,132,000 felony convictions in state courts:

- 18 percent were violent offenses including murder, sexual assault, aggravated assault, and robbery
- 28 percent were related to property, including burglary, larceny, and fraud
- 33 percent were related to drugs, either possession or trafficking
- 21 percent were classified as "other"
- 83 percent or so are men, the balance of 17 percent women

Figure No: 19

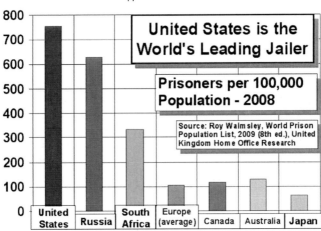

These observations have nothing to do with the quality of law enforcement or the brave men that wear those badges and protect our interest and lives daily. They are subjected to our court systems and various rules that for many of us make no sense, especially those of us who were affected by a crime. Let's face it, it's broke and needs to be fixed.

The United States military is one of the most impressive organizations in the world. Hell, we all know that a toilet bowl doesn't cost $345.00 when we hear about examples of questionable military spending, and we all chuckle when the topic is raised. But Americans love their soldiers, and they understand this government entity has historical significance and ensures we maintain our freedoms and quality of life.

The most effective way to pay a debt to society is not to rot in some prison, or be part of the failing system, it is to defend it and be active in the pursuit of that defense. It's honorable, and for many prisoners, it may subject them to additional skills and a better understanding of what it means to be an American.

We will close the prisons and place the inmates into the USA military.

During this engagement in the military, as in prison, wages would be reduced to prison wage to $800 per month. Assuming the average US soldier's pay is $4000 per month, that would save $38,400 per year time for the 1.6 million inmates, or $61 billion in service pay. In addition, it would reduce prison costs by $30 billion a year and free up the real estate with a total impact of almost $100 billion per year. The thought that a criminal would have to go to combat and put his or her life in harm's way would be a significant deterrent and would most likely reduce crime by 50 percent, thus reducing the savings accordingly.

1776 LLC EXECUTIVE MANAGEMENT TEAM

CEO: HEARN: "Okay, we have 2.2 million people incarcerated for any number of crimes, and we need to fix this thing. Incarcerations have increased five times since 1980, costs are in excess of $65 billion to house and feed these inmates, and upon their release, there is a good change that many will return. This thing is broken, and the costs are skyrocketing. The percentage of inmates returning back to prison is out of control, and we have some good real estate tied up in a failing business model. Brian has the manufacturing and operations guys looked at this from a logistics perspective?"

VP MANUFACTURING: YOUNG: "We have 2.2 million people incarcerated in one form or another, broken into four major groups. Of these, 18 percent are violent offenses; 29 percent are in robbery; 33 percent are drug-related; and the balance in "other." Our plan to remedy this is defined as "Operation Cell Soldier". My first overhead list the general types of crimes and where these cell soldiers would be assigned:

Operation Cell Soldier: Assignment of Duties

1. Violent offenders will be on the front lines and trained for house to house assignments, mine field clearings, and first offensive maneuvers.

2. Robbery and theft will be assigned to Special Forces who will train these folks on stealing the enemy supplies, robbing ammunition from the enemy, and pilfering their ammunition depots.

3. Drug-related inmates will also be a Special Forces unit that manufacturer and sell field-prepared drugs to enemy combatants to assist in demoralizing their forces and help them stay inebriated.

4. White collar crime inmates will be assigned to accounting and administrative tasks and find international sources of funds that provide resources to the enemy and reinvest those funds in sham investments to reduce the inflow of cash to the enemy.

5. Rapists, child molesters, those who commit incest and those types of criminals will be placed in latrine duty and garbage detail and kitchen duty."

Chris Murtagh

YOUNG: "Assuming we did execute a plan for this scheme, the training and facility requirements would be huge. First we have to get these guys in shape. Boot camp would be doubled in length and intensity, training would be focused on selecting the candidates by specific learned expertise, and then exploit that to the strategies we have in place for defense. We would also want an exit strategy so that these inmates are trained for a specific civilian trade or profession, so when they leave the military, they have sufficient training to land a job. In addition, as veterans, employers would be provided with certain incentives to hire these new civilians. Minimum time in the military would be five years. Of those five years; it would include one year boot camp training, three years active duty, and one year civilian training."

VP FINANCE: DARBON: "While the data varies based upon Federal or State or local prison, we will use a baseline monthly salary payment these inmates get paid now at $100 per month or $0.62 an hour. Average combat pay including all allowances for today's military is about $3000 per month (excluding any life and health insurance premiums). Since they are still incarcerated, we would save the equivalent of $2900 per month, or $34,800 per year times 2.2 million, or $77 billion a year. If we only focus on 80 percent of the population (assuming the juveniles and elderly could not serve), then we are looking at about $62 billion per year in savings.

"The cost, however, for training these inmates would be an additional $5 billion ongoing overhead; with one time expanded services and facilities costs of another $15 billion, so we are still ahead by about $40 billion a year in savings.

"If the white collar guys could find out where the international drug funds flow and how and where the terrorist funds flow, we could start an investment scam, have those funds invested into some bogus scam operation, and pick up another $10-15 billion to assist in offsetting these costs. Let's get that Bernie Madoff guy working for the shareholders instead of rotting in some prison cell.

"We save $40 billion a year in salary, save $65 billion a year in correctional facility costs, and have the potential of picking up another $10-$15 billion through elaborate investment scams from rouge nations."

VP MARKETING: BRINSTER: "Our market studies show that if future inmates are faced with the option of going to county jail for one to two years or the military for five years, the crime incident rates would drop by about 60 percent. Our defense would be at record-level preparedness, and the quality of these inmates returning to society after the career training programs would put these previous inmates to work as carpenters, plumbers, police officers, and other trades or professionals. Our studies show the following professions following military service:

> ### Operation Cell Soldier: Return from Duty
>
> 1. Police officers and law enforcement, about 25-30 percent
> 2. Building trades, carpenters, plumbers, welders, about 15 percent
> 3. Professionals, including engineers and accountants, about 15 percent
> 4. Medical industry, about 10 percent
> 5. Communication and IT-focused, about 20 percent
> 6. Balance would be career military, about 10 percent

"Compared with an approximate 50 percent return-to-prison rate, these 2 million people or so would earn about $70,000 per year or $140 billion with tax revenues to the government of about $42 billion per year."

VP BUSINESS DEVELOPMENT: GETHER: "Do you know how much real estate we have tied up in these prisons and the underlying value it has to the owners of the real estate, the shareholders? If you figure around 400 square feet of actual building per inmate (80 square feet for the cell and the balance of 320 square feet for the eating and recreation areas along with prison staff), that's close to 800 million square feet of buildings. Figuring, conservatively, a 50 percent ratio of building to land provides us with 1.6 Billion square feet of land or around 37,000 acres of land that directly houses the inmates. At even $100 per square foot of existing finished building structures, that's $800 Billion tied up in real estate alone. I would estimate the value more toward $1 Trillion. In business, gentlemen as we all know, when one has a $1 Trillion asset with no return on that investment, the buildings and land needs to be reinvested in higher growing businesses. I suggest we take those funds and use them to invest in shareholder growth and reassign this business model to the military that is far more capable of adding value to these inmates as compared to letting them rot in some confined space and assume they are rehabilitated."

CEO: HEARN: "So we reduce spending from $65 billion to about $15 billion for existing correctional facility programs, reduce solider pay for inmates by around $62 billion per year, reduce new inmates by 60 percent, sell the real estate for $ 1 Trillion and exit with 2 million or so inmates earning approximately $140 Billion per year. The initial costs would be around $20 billion but would be a pay-as-you-go, especially if those white collar guys could bring in additional $10-$15 billion in these scam investments from rogue nations. I do not know of any other option on the table now that can turn around this failing business unit, reduce operating costs and increase revenues that significantly. Jeff, do you have a preliminary budget?"

VP FINANCE: DARBON: "Gentlemen, referring to the attached slide you see before you, there is considerable upside in the plan. I broke the tables into four portions.

Table 7A-7D outlines the investments to be made to move these 2.0 Million convicts from the prison system to the military, ongoing costs savings and proceeds back to the shareholders to support investments."

Table No: 7A Investments for Operation Cell Soldier: One Time Costs

Item	Budget (ea)	Total Budget
Transfer 2 Million inmates to military	$5,000	$10 Billion
Expand military facilities.	$40,000	$80 Billion
Close prisons	$2000	$5 Billion
Total onetime costs		**$95 Billion**

Table No: 7B Investments for Operation Cell Soldier: Ongoing Costs

Item	Existing	Revised	Savings
Reduce prison overhead	$65 Billion	$15 Billion	$40 Billion
Solider Pay: 2 Million	$72 Billion	$2 Billion	$70 Billion
Increase military overhead: 10,000 military supervisors	$0	$2 Billion	($2 Billion)
Other			($2 Billion)
Total Ongoing Costs			**$110 Billion**

Table No: 7C Sale of Prison Assets

Item	Value
800 Million Square Feet	$ 1 Trillion

Table No: 7D Overall Effect

Item	Budget	Proceeds
Sale of Property	$1 Trillion	$1 Trillion
Investments :One Time Costs	$95 Billion	($95 Billion)
Savings: Ongoing Costs	$110 Billion	$110 Billion
Proceeds to shareholders		**$1.015 Trillion**

CEO: HEARN: "I see no other course here except to divest this business model and I agree the military is the most effective method to deal with this. In addition to the deterrent this may offer to future criminals, it adds the benefit of having these inmates contribute to society by defending it and returning to society with training and developments in areas of strong employment where it can further contribute to society instead of 50-60% of them returning back to prison. Have your guys drive down into the numbers and give me the overall contribution and, oh-by the way-don't forget about the additional $10-$15 Billion from those white collar guys"

Prison systems and methods of incarceration have evolved over the years. Many blame society, lack of family structure and other

*events that affect the growth of prison population. Poor educa-
tion, family abuse, greed and other factors drive many of the basic
root causes that require elevated societies to change their position
regarding how to handle criminals. The decision the shareholders
made in the past and make today regarding how to handle its
prison population have, however, resulted in skyrocketing prison
population and even worse, a high rate of return to prison life.
Nationalized TV shows now take us inside prison life on a daily
basis. Watching these shows and witnessing men and women sit-
uated within a unique lifestyle and culture and rotting away in a
prison cell is challenging as it wears on the shareholders ability to
invest in its future growth. The shareholders can no longer afford
these social experiments whose results show dismal success. 1776
LLC management team is focused on growth and does not dif-
ferentiate between the sociological aspects of experimenting with
the lives of criminals against its hope or trust that something will
change things. The criminal justice system is broken and needs to
be fixed. It does however; challenge the shareholder in maintaining a system that drains the life out of its society by extorting
needed funds for growth by supporting business models that do
not work. Given the poor results to date along with most forecasts
of expenditures yet to come, the shareholders need to address these
issues or will continue with this human and financial drain that
appear to be defining the new US charter.*

CHAPTER 4

NOPEC
$ 532,000,000,000

"The Christians had a better chance against the lions than the American consumer has against the OPEC cartel.

—Ed Markey

According to the EIA (Energy Information Administration) the USA consumes approximately 140 Billion gallons of gasoline each year. At an average price of $3.80 per gallon, the annual money spent for gasoline is $532 billion based upon current (2010-2011) estimates of prices at the pump. The USA shareholders are getting ready to respond to the skyrocketing oil prices that plague this economy and finally put an end to the fossil fuel era.

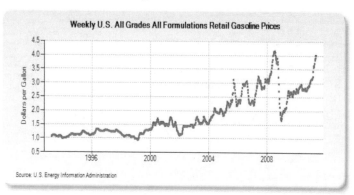

Weekly U.S. All Grades All Formulations Retail Gasoline Prices

Source: U.S. Energy Information Administration

What were we thinking? Did we really expect the US consumer to tolerate the pilfer aging at the pump?

We are entering into a new world of electric cars. Electric vehicles are seen as a major step toward controlling gas emissions, less dependence on foreign oil, and freedom from the pumps. We can plug our cars in at home, charge the batteries, and skip the pump lines. What would be the result of an aggressive campaign to replace these fossil fuel guzzlers with electric cars?

1. The good news is the USA power plants will get the benefit of revenues on a local basis, with less oil imports from overseas. We like that. Keep the money home, here in the USA. Good for employment and good for the economy.

2. Consumption of oil will be reduced at local oil refineries, and imports will decline. Bad news for

the refinery guys, but they will move their jobs to the power companies, so we may break even on that employment exchange.

3. Gasoline prices will eventually fall below $1.00 per gallon as demand for oil decreases for gas engines. The oil companies will be at the tables in Washington, DC, by 2020, looking for bailout funds.

4. The construction of new power plants to keep up with the demand of electric cars will skyrocket, bringing more local construction and utility jobs into the marketplace. Good, we like that. Great for the local economy.

5. Gas stations will convert to something else as the electric car quietly drives by them every day and no longer needing that form of energy. The less efficient gasoline era will go the way of the dinosaur (again, no pun intended). Can't really use these facilities anymore. There are approximately 120,000 gas stations in the USA that employ about four persons each for an estimated 480,000 jobs, not including the oil trucks and transfer stations. About 92 percent are attached to convenience stores. Hey, what about the marijuana guys? I think they need around 85,000 new retail centers, and these gas stations are at perfect locations.

6. In time, the gasoline engine will be replaced with an electric or other type of motor, sparking exciting expansion into new technologies and, if orchestrated properly and with a little pain, move the USA into new areas.

7. Manufacturing plants for battery technology will increase significantly.
8. Better sell off your oil-changing and gas station business now.

The largest importer of petroleum products in 2009 to the USA are Canada and Mexico, whose daily imports total 2,447,000 and 1,237,000 barrels respectively per day, followed by Venezuela at 1,099,000 and then Saudi Arabia at 1,023,000.

Unfortunately, these folks will feel most of the pain. As the imports start to decline and transportation moves from oil to electric motor (or other kinds of power), the USA market will decline in its use of their products and services and replace them with home-grown local power plants, putting an end to an era of oil imports.

The market response will be a significant decline in gasoline prices as the electric motor-driven vehicle, batteries, and associated components increase in popularity, driving down oil and gas consumption.

At an average round trip of 40 miles per day, costs for gasoline estimated at $5-6/day will drop to $1.50 per day, or the equivalent of $0.75 a gallon for gasoline.

If the shareholders could expedite those changes the annual costs of gasoline would decline from today's levels of $532 Billion a year to around $106 Billion a year providing after tax shareholder cash in pocket of $426 Billion a year in hard cash or approximately $1716 for each of the 310 million shareholders. The shareholders ability to pump that

$426 Billion per year back into the economy from this single initiative plus increasing employment at the power plant levels and reducing its dependency on foreign oil is staggering. Imagine the effect of putting 50 Million of these new electric cars on the road in the next 5 years?

HISTORY OF GASOLINE PRICES

The price for gasoline at the pump rose 50% in the eight year period starting at 1992 at $1.00 per gallon to $1.50 a gallon in the year 2000. What happened in the following 8 years from 2000-2008 that caused the same price levels to increase 173% from $1.50 per gallon in 2000 to $4.10 per gallon in 2008? What decisions were made to drive the price of gasoline at such a significant rate? Did the global oil supply significantly change? Taxes increase? The cost to refine oil to gasoline went through the ceiling? Consumption outpaced demand? Do you know why? The pace of oil industry mergers and acquisitions from 1998-2001 is legendary and represents one of the broadest consolidations for a single industry. Total oil industry revenues in 1997, as an example, were approximately $1.45 Trillion. The combined merger and acquisition activities of the following companies represent approximately $848 Billion or 57% of the entire industry, at that time.

Major Oil Company Mergers: 1998-2001 [15]

Combined Companies	Combined Revenues(millions)
BP/Amoco	$123,871
Total/PetroFina	$53,133
Exxon/Mobil	$203,148
BP Amoco/ARCO	$143,143
TotalFina/Elf Aquitaine	$98,220
Chevron/Texaco	$88,617
Phillips/Tosco	$43,870
Conoco/Gulf Canada	$22,622
Phillips/Conoco	$66,492
Total	$848,116

The coincidence of this level of industry consolidation followed by an eight year explosive growth in gasoline pricing may be that simple; only a coincidence. As the real estate and stock market started its declines in 2006-2007, investors diverted their funds into the commodity markets of which oil is a major component. In addition, the declining value of the US dollar caused overseas suppliers to increase price levels to offset the currency devaluation and "poof" a perfect storm was created. Driven more by commodity speculation as compared to actual supply and demand; oil price fluctuations now are based upon a significant number of factors outside of the historical supply and demand issues of yesteryear.

It appears the shareholders themselves carry a partial burden of this responsibility as it was the shareholders money

---

15   http://www.anderson.ucla.edu/faculty/john.weston/papers/exxonmerger.pdf

that was moved from real estate and stock market declines into the commodity markets and not only oil. Gold, wheat, food prices and other commodities increased significantly in a short period of time.

Oil industry consolidation activities of the late 1990's assisted oil companies in recent booming profits. These consolidations increased efficiencies, reduced overhead, reduced competition and increased prices at the pump providing the oil industry with record profits.

If, however, investor funds that found their way to the commodity markets were spoofed into believing that oil was going the way of the dinosaur driven by alternate fuel technologies, if demand, still a strong underlying pricing force, were forecast to drop by 30% in a short timeframe and if the shareholders really wanted to put an end to dependence upon OPEC to determine the future of oil pricing that effect their economic viability and their pursuit of happiness, then the shareholders themselves can drive this change.

1776 LLC EXECUTIVE MANAGEMENT TEAM

CEO: HEARN: "What the hell have they done to themselves? They import oil from other nations (some that mean them harm), and raped the shareholders by increasing gas at the pump, over the past several years, from $2.00 a gallon to $4.00 a gallon. That difference amounts to $280 billion in one year alone. Are we out of our minds? Come-on now!

VP MANUFACTURING: YOUNG: "I agree, sir. This thing got out of hand. We were drilling all over the place, and the BP leak in the Gulf has really messed things up. We had our heads up our butts and lost sight of the fundamental 'come-on' cents rules. A major difficulty is at the refining areas. Our refineries are aging. The last one we built was back in 1976. In addition, we had about 300 refineries back in the early 1980s, and through consolidations are at less than half of that now. If I recall, our last count was 149 operating refineries. They spent close to $50 billion over the past ten to fifteen years in cleaning up the existing refineries, making them more efficient and reducing pollutants, but the capacity to refine is limited to around 9-10 million barrels of oil per day. Hell, in ten to fifteen years, they will need to refine 12-13 million barrels of oil, and they just do not have the infrastructure to do that. They are operating at around 80-85 percent plant utilization, and their refineries do not make the oil companies a whole lot of money. I have no clue what these shareholders are thinking. They want inexpensive gasoline; they delay or deny permits for new refining facilities, and the price of oil is no longer a supply and demand issue as much as a commodity trading issue. I like the idea of shifting from traders that set the price of oil and high refinery manufacturing costs to electric motor vehicles. But I want these motor vehicles powered by solar collectors mounted in people's homes. In addition, we will have to wean off the oil, and I suggest our first pass is with the gas/electric vehicle combination in the shorter term. The markets will then react and eventually conclude that newer technologies will be developed, including hydrogen-powered fuel cell cars. In addition, there is a growing shift to natural gas engines in the larger truck industries that significantly reduce emissions.

VP MARKETING: BRINSTER: "The shareholders invested money into the electric car development and launched that in 2011. Their product managers expect sales to be 100-150,000 units by 2015 and an annual growth of 10-15 percent per year following that. The government entities provided tax credits of $7000 per vehicle to assist in the initial launch. The automotive guys are saying they can have production up to 50-60,000 units by 2012. That should assist in putting a slight dent in gasoline consumption but that is nickel-and-dime stuff. I want to replace the entire postal service and other federal government vehicles that are estimated at 350,000 cars and the local state police and other vehicles with estimated cars of 600,000 and get 1 million new vehicles on the road immediately in 2012. Let stop this one-at-a-time crap and get into the meat of it. These government service vehicles operate eight to ten hours a day, and most absorb 6 gallons of gas a day, or about $4 million a day in gas or $1.4 billion a year. The sooner we get going on populating the USA market with these electric cars, the sooner gasoline prices will drop for the balance of cars on the road. We have 480,000 school buses in the

USA sucking up 825 million gallons of diesel at $2.0 billion dollars. Hell, public transportation buses put on around 45 billion miles a year between them, and that's got to be worth around $20 billion in diesel and gasoline itself. We need the guys in R&D to come up with a retrofit program to retool these buses and reduce the annual tab for fuel by $ $10-15 billion."

"I like our earlier idea of importing the 80 million new consumers and providing these 13 million households with 26 million new electric-driven cars in the first five years. If business development can get us of these government sponsored nonperforming businesses and loosen up some cash, we may have an answer. But to think that production of 60-100,000 units a year is meaningful in the short term is ridiculous. The CEO reminded us that these 1776 shareholders have a unique tendency to get together in crises. I suggest we declare war on oil, fire up the factories, get production going, get solar panels installed in each home to charge up the batteries, and drop oil and gas production by 30 percent in five years, followed by the balance in the next ten years. Get 5 million electric cars a year, over the next five years, on the road to support the new imported consumers and another 5 million a year to replace some of the 250 million cars on the road today. That's 50 million electric powered cars on the road by 2016. We will refer to this initiative as "NOPEC"

VP FINANCE: DARBON: "If these NOPEC numbers the marketing guys are boasting are true, then the round trip costs per day of electricity for 40 miles would be $1.50. The present-day cost for the consumer is around $4-5 per day. The consumer saves $3.00 per day of approximately $1000 per year. That is the equivalent of gas prices at $0.75 per gallon. The threat alone would drive gas prices down immediately, affecting the balance of gasoline cars on the road today. We have approximately 250 million cars in the USA, spending $532 billion a year at $3.80 per gallon. If gas prices were driven to $1.00 per gallon, quickly, the immediate savings at the pump would be about $300 billion in the consumer's pocket. We need a bold program supported with a full court press on this, as this single action would pull us out of the recession. According to the HIS Production Barometer, US light auto production averaged around 10-12 million units per year over the past several years. We are looking at a 50% increase in auto production over the next 5-10 years to get these additional 50 Million cars on the road."

VP HUMAN RESOURCE: BLACKWELL: "I am concerned about the lost jobs in the USA, especially in the oil and gasoline side. As the electric car comes into play, the shareholder's oil industry will be hit hard, and the unemployment may be offset by this power industry or solar industry guys if we put solar power into the homes of the 50 million new cars planned for the next five years. I do believe, in the short term, that lowing gas prices will still keep them busy at the pump, but at a reduced rate. A great majority of the oil supply side is offshore and does not affect the employment to the same extent. I think the auto industry boasts it employs about 800,000 workers directly, with an indirect effect of another 3 million workers or so. If we increase new automobile output by 50% that would require an additional 2 million auto company related workers, direct and indirect, dropping unemployment from 9 percent to around 8 percent from this move alone."

VP BUSINESS DEVELOPMENT: GETHER: "Guys, as Caesar said, 'The die has been cast.' The impact of the electric vehicle and reduction on oil is sound. Let's look at the benefits from this initiative. If you could turn your attention to the overhead, I summarized the discussion regarding NOPEC benefits as follows:

Benefits of NOPEC

1. Oil consumption in the USA will drop 30 percent in the next ten years if we move boldly and enhance the purchase of these vehicles.
2. Reduction in offshore oil revenues will drive down influence from our OPEC nations and bring peace worldwide.
3. Pollution will decline significantly, and costly offshore drilling will cease due to reduction in demand, especially when solar panels are recharging these batteries.

---

4. Revenues for electric demand will shift to the power companies that are all domestic and employ US workers.

5. Construction will increase in the USA for new power plants.

6. Consumer transportation related expenses will be reduced by hundreds of billions of dollars and pumped right back into the economy.

7. Oil companies will focus on domestic production and cease imports.

8. Government tax revenues will increase due to reduction in oil and increased consumer spending.

9. Solar power will require upgrading 20 million households to support the electric car. No doubt this will be further integrated into the balance of the existing homes.

10. The new home construction guys will standardize on solar panels to capture this market shift. After we populate the 13 million vacant homes with new 80 Million consumers, the housing market will come back more powerful than ever, with each new home supporting solar power.

11. Hotels, motels, parking garages, and office parks will also convert to solar power with this monumental effort to support their employees.

12. The list goes on and on. We cannot depend upon government service guys to set the tone. Hell, most of these guys are lawyers and have no clue about business, except for hourly billings.

"This reminds me of the WW2 efforts when the factories were operating at full steam based upon a single purpose: support-the-war efforts. I agree with Brinster. Move boldly, get over 1 million of these new electric vehicles on the road in year one and shoot for the 50 million a year by 2016. The USA converted factories and developed new products at lightning speed during WW2 and did so understanding its liberty and freedom were at stake. Well, guys, it's at stake now. Economic freedom and economic stability ensure they can sustain freedom. High debt and higher unemployment and lack of direction, cause for frustration. Stop the nonsense with our PR guys in Washington screwing around and pointing fingers. This one directive will get everyone on the same path. Declare war on oil, declare war on emissions, declare war on rogue nations that finance our destruction, and get bold on this electric car thing. The impact is greater than you think. Get the guys focused."

VP R&D: THORPE: "Gentlemen, the plan sounds exciting. My concern is that the electricity used to charge these car batteries are supported by local power plants, of which 50 percent are sourced by coal-fired plants that drive carbon emissions at a higher rate than the gasoline engine, and higher sulfur dioxides at twice the rate than the gasoline engine. We need to address the coal-fired plants that support 50 percent of the USA electricity generation if we are to move from gasoline to electricity overnight.

Figure No: 21 Fossil Fuel Emission Levels Pounds

Pollutant	Natural Gas	Oil	Coal
Carbon Dioxide	117,000	164,000	208,000
Carbon Monoxide	40	33	208
Nitrogen Oxide	92	448	457
Sulfur Dioxides	1	1,122	2,591
Particulates	7	84	2,744
Mercury	0.00	0.007	0.016

THORPE: "In addition, our power plants generate approximately 45-50 Exajoules of electricity but only 13-14 Exajoules find their way to local residences and other users. We lose 70 percent of fuel resources in the generation and transmission of power in the electrical system grid. The aggressive move to remove gasoline from the fuel source and replace it with electric-generated cars would lower dependence on foreign oil but pollute the environment at a higher pace, given the existing power infrastructure, especially east of the Mississippi, where we have almost 75 percent of all coal-fired plants in the USA. When we last checked, there were around 1500 coal-fired plants in the USA.

"We agree that the solution is in increasing use of solar power at each residence where, upon the purchase of the electric car, a solar panel kit will be installed in each residence to provide the overnight charging of these batteries. We would also promote the use at parking garages, work locations, and use the private sector as the kickoff to help offset these anticipated uses. I would keep it away from the government guys, as they would make a seven-course meal out of this sandwich, over regulate, and try to add some value and screw the thing up." The data is compelling. Let's take this technology, fund it, and get going on changing the direction of 1776, LLC. "

CEO: HEARN: "Okay then, we have consensus. Let's summarize those as follows:

Operation NOPEC Initiatives Summary

1. We will move boldly on the electric car strategy and declare war on oil. Fifty million new electric cars in the next five years. Twenty-six million for the new 80 Million imported consumers, and 24 million replaced gas-guzzlers.
2. We will push for 50 percent of all new car sales to be electric cars by 2020.
3. Oil prices should decline to $1.00 per gallon by 2014.
4. We will replace all gasoline government vehicles during 2013-2015, no exceptions.
5. We get the R&D guys figuring out the retrofit for the bus systems.
6. We will get some solar support in the private sector

CEO: HEARN: "Jeff, can we see some preliminary budget and return numbers for this initiative?

VP FINANCE: DARBON: "I've been designing the spreadsheets as we speak and these may be a little rough but should set the tone and give an indication of the impact of this initiative:

Table No: 8A NOPEC Campaign Budget: 5 Year Overview

Initiative	Objective	Budget (ea)	Total Annual Budget	Tax Revenues (5%)
24 Million Cars	Replace gas guzzlers	$30,000	$720 Billion	$0
24 Gas Guzzlers	Sell to export countries	$3000	($75 Billion)	$0
24 Million Cars	Purchase-50%	($15,000)	($360 Billion)	$18 Billion
25 Million solar	Solar Panel home installations	$2500	$63 Billion	$3 Billion
5 Year Budget			**$348 Billion**	**$21 Billion**

DARBON: "Table No: 8A outlines the budget of $348 Billion with $21 Billion in local sales tax at an average rate of 5% of the 50% discounted car price. We will provide a 50% discount for the first 24 Million vehicles and let the States decide the criteria for those purchases. We will require those car buyers to purchase solar panels reducing dependency on power plants.

"Table No: 8B, our next slide outlines the impact on employment and associated tax revenues with this initiative."

Table No: 8B NOPEC Campaign: 5 Year Salary Contribution Overview

Initiative	Objective	Salary	Tax revenues: 30%
Employment	2 Million auto workers/year	$160 Billion	$48 Billion
Employment (loss)	100,000 gas station workers/year	($4 Billion)	($0.12 Billion)
Solar Power Manufacturer	250,000 manufacturing/year	$18 Billion	$5 Billion
Solar Panel Installers	250,000 contractors/year	$12 Billion	$4 Billion
Other	Varies/Contingency	$5 Billion	$2 Billion
Total/Year		**$191 Billion**	**$57 Billion**
Five Year Total		**$955 Billion**	**$286 Billion**

DARBON: "Slide No: 8C includes revenues expected from the business side along with gasoline savings and pumped back into the economy over the five year period.

Table No: 8C NOPEC Campaign: Tax Revenues

Initiative	Forecast	Tax Rate	Tax revenues
Revenues from Auto Industry	$720 Billion	30%	$216 Billion
Revenues from Solar Manufacture	$43 Billion	30%	$13 Billion
Revenues from Solar Contractors	$20 Billion	30%	$6 Billion
Gas Savings: 50 Million Cars: 20MPG	$142 Billion	5% (Sales Tax)	$7 Billion
Total	$925 Billion		$242 Billion

DARBON: "The return on this five year investment includes the summary highlights in Table 1D. I suggest we set our expectations at 1/2 of what Table No: 8D shows until we get everyone together and work out the details-but it is interesting."

Table No: 8D NOPEC Investments and Returns

Item	Overview	Investment ($Return)
24 Million Cars	Five Year production	$720 Billion
24 Million solar panels	Five Year production	$63 Billion
Total Investment		**$783 Billion**
Sale of gas guzzlers-Export		($75 Billion)
50% Discount Revenues		($360 Billion)
Salary Tax Revenues		($286 Billion)
Corp Revenues		($242 Billion)
Total Revenues		($963 Billion)
Return on Investment		**$180 Billion**

CEO: HEARN: "Great job guys! Jeff, I think you may want to add the expected price decline of gasoline of $1-$2.00 per gallon over the period as well for the balance of the 200 Million cars or so still on the highway. We also need to include employment from the construction industry that will need to add about 1-2 Billion square feet of new auto manufacturing facilities and the tax revenues from that initiative. The auto guys will fund that expansion on their nickel if they know we will "pony-up" the $15,000 per car. We are making good progress here. We have identified grow areas in adding 80 Million new consumers, putting 25 Million new electric vehicles on the road, reduced cost and expense in the prison system and are balancing the growth plan with cost reductions in non-performing assets. The addition of $783 Billion in GDP for the NOPEC initiative and $400 Billion in the "Weed-Out America" campaign and $3.8 Trillion in GDP for the "Grow America Campaign" bringing up to a total of 19.98 Trillion GDP, with cost reductions of around $1 Trillion for the "Operation Cell Soldier". We are balancing growth with cost reductions. We're going to need some cash flow to support these initiatives over the first five years and I look to hear more on that in the next session".

VP FINANCE: DARBON: "Hang on there John. I trust we're still considering an underlying 2% annual growth in baseline $15 Trillion GDP. That would be added to these incremental growth plans with baseline growth of $1.6 Trillion getting us to $21.6 Trillion in year 5 after the kick-off."

CEO: HEARN: "Jeff, I smell another $1-2 Trillion in gains we have not really measured in these initiatives." Find me the additional $2 Trillion and I'll even throw in a 2% annual inflation for the initiatives to get us to the $25 Trillion in year 7. Fair enough?"

VP FINANCE: DARBON: "Fair enough!"

CEO: HEARN: "Gene, we are also looking forward to these cost reductions you mention earlier. We are projecting about $1 Trillion from the "Operation Cell Solider" initiatives. I'd feel better if we could find another $3-4 Trillion hidden in the "black hole". Oh and by the way, I want to see if we can wipe out this $15 Trillion debt thing over the next 7 years. Makes it easier to start clean in 2017; gives the shareholders a little wiggle room. See you guys in the morning."

These "come-on" cents discussions and debates focus on increasing the strength and vitality of the US economy. It has no concern about political issues, overseas interests, or pressure on existing business. The horse and buggy gave way to the car, oil gives way to electricity, and eventually electric cars will give way to new technologies and methods of transportation. Unfortunately, Saudi Arabia, Venezuela, Iran, Iraq, Canada, Mexico, and other oil-producing countries will feel the sting of the American consumer as it reduces its worldwide consumption of oil by 50 percent in the year 2030. These once lovely, posh deserts will return to their wilderness days as oil derricks are removed from the landscape and replaced with golf courses. Funds that have flowed from many of these nations to support financial terror groups will be reduced or eliminated, consumer spending will increase substantially, and the USA will lead the world in technological developments as it wrestles with transportation, long overdue.

We Americans, however, are a resilient group. Just imagine the price at the pump of $1.00 per gallon of gasoline, and 30% of our drivers using electric vehicles by 2017 and using solar power to charge these batteries? The thought of cars using natural gas, where America has a 100 year supply, which reduces emissions by 20-25% as compared to gasoline, is awesome; but it requires renewed focus and an understanding of what these visions mean to each shareholder. The only thing that is in the way of these ideas actually becoming reality is the shareholders themselves. The government service segment of the shareholders group needs to be pushed by the shareholders to actually do something and change its perspective on areas of investment and areas of overhead.

CHAPTER 5

OBMD: ORBIT BASED MISSILE DEFENSE
$1,291,000,000,000

You cannot help men permanently by doing for them what they could and should do for themselves.

Abraham Lincoln

In case this number is too large to understand, the total displayed is $1.29 trillion spent on the war in Iraq and Afghanistan since its inception, and forecast through the end of 2011. According to the Congressional Research Service Report RL33110 p-CRS-9 approximately $802 billion was for Iraq, $456 billion was for Afghanistan, and the balance, of $34 Billion for enhanced security and "other".

Figure No: 21 Cost of Wars in Afghanistan & Iraq 2001-2011F ($ Billions)[17]

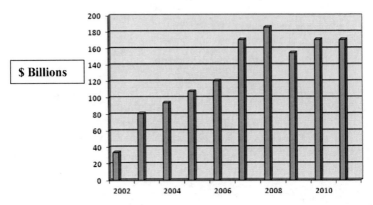

As comparison, the Vietnam War lasted approximately ten years and cost the USA taxpayers $584 billion and lost 58,159 American lives. The Korean War lasted three years and cost the taxpayers $20 billion and lost 54,000 American lives. World War Two lasted six years and cost the taxpayers, at that time, $288 billion, which is approximately equal to $3.4 trillion in today's money, and lost 405,000 American lives.

This book does not look at the moral implications, reasons for going to war, effects on humanity, or other social or political challenges. It merely looks at past decisions and tries to measure their present-day impact. Let's take a quick review:

---

17 http://www.fas.org/sgp/crs/natsec/RL33110.pdf

1. World War Two addressed German and Japanese dictators, ended in their defeat, provided world peace, and made America a leading contributor to sustaining that peace. Today Germany and Japan are world innovators of technical products, world business leaders, and strong allies with the USA. That war lasted six years, and the peace between the USA and its previous foes has lasted over sixty years.

2. The Korean War addressed aggression from North Korea and ended in a settlement dividing Korea as America withdrew after a three-year period. Today North Korea, lead by a wacko leader, still toys with the peace and security of the region and recently attacked a South Korean ship, with American politicians settling on "saber-rattling" and threats of embargos. Poor return for the American shareholder on the $20 billion investment, and there is never a return for the lives lost in battle.

3. The Vietnam War, previously the longest war in American history, killed 58,159 Americans, cost the taxpayers $584 billion, and left a line in the sand separating North from South Vietnam.

4. The war on terror in the combined countries of Afghanistan and Iraq is the longest military conflict in the history of the USA with regime change in both countries a major driver for these recent conflicts.

It would be disrespectful on the part of this author to minimize any American life lost or wounded in these battles, as there is no one soldier's life lost that should go without merit, gratitude, and thanks to these soldiers and support staff that gave more than can be summarized in this book. Those costs can never be recouped, and we thank them and our present and past day soldiers for defending our nation, even if we disagree or point out flaws in the government decision-making during these battles. On the contrary, this book attempts to make us all think clearly about the decision of putting these fine soldiers in harm's way and looks to the past to guide us in the future.

The shareholders made a decision, years ago, to become the police force for the world and provide an unusual service by maintaining strong military presence in many countries. That presence, in most circumstances, acts as a deterrent to many rogue nations. Is this business model outdated? I mean, do we really need bases in Germany, Japan, and other friendly places around the world? What are the costs to operate these? Do the local countries pay for this police force, or is this a freebie?

According to the US Department of Defense "Base Structure Report-Fiscal Year 2010", the US Military operates in over 2 billion square feet of space, worldwide, with 361 Million square feet located overseas-or around 17% of the total. The inventory of buildings and facilities owned and leased by the Department of Defense (excuse me; the shareholders) is shown in Table No: 1

Table No: 9 US Department of Defense Global Active Base Structures 2010 Fiscal Year Report Square Foot in millions

Location	Square Foot Owned	Square Foot Leased	Square Foot-Other	Total Square Foot
USA	1,520,203,021	38,048,064	250,965,510	1,809,216,585
Overseas	143,152,554	22,507,395	195,649,484	361,309,443
Total	1,663,355,575	60,555,459	446,614,994	2,170,526,028

Of the 361 Million square feet of overseas buildings and facilities owned and leased the majority- 86%- of these are located in Europe, Japan and South Korea.

Table No: 10 Overseas Military Facilities Square Foot in millions

Country	Square Foot Active	% Total
United Kingdom	17	5%
Japan	115	32%
Germany	132	37%
South Korea	47	13%
Other	50	14%
Total	361 Million	100%

The shareholder's decision to fund a global police force is in question. Many would argue that the investment, while painful, is insurance against future wars and a major deterrent to nations that plan harm to the shareholders. Others argue that the USA should not be the global police force, especially when those insurance costs are so high that the shareholders can't pay for their $15 Trillion mortgage that, in turn weakens the nation. How can the shareholders invest in tomorrow's technology with its economy crumbling and burdened with $15 Trillion in debt, exporting its previous manufactured goods overseas that now includes a deficient with China at almost $3 Trillion since 1985, and its unemployment at near record levels, its population aging and its medical bills skyrocketing?

Freedom, prosperity, and the American way of life were driven internally by citizens of the 13 colonies who pledged their lives and fortunes in declaring independence from a tyrannical government. It was further sustained, internally, during the Civil War when, again, shareholder's put their lives on the line to maintain the 1776 charter. It invested in expansion, infrastructure and defended its liberties and freedom in great world wars all for the sake of maintaining its way of life without outside influences and without external regime changes.

Overthrowing a foreign government in Iraq, however, that never asked for these principles, and showing to millions of their inhabitants a "follow me, boys" drive for independence and freedom that most do not understand, and thinking it will be successful, are still to be realized. Feeding a man in time of need is charity and results in immediate gratification for all parties. Planting corn in a man's fields so that he can feed himself may be detrimental to all parties since the man who received the corn did so without the knowledge of the burden entailed in the planting and harvesting of that corn and will never be able to sustain the cornfield.

The tab for the war in Iraq and Afghanistan estimated at $1.3 Trillion (if the US exits by the end of 2011) may eventually reach $1.7 Trillion when it is finally complete or slightly less than 50% of the cost of World War Two in today's dollars of $3.8 Trillion. Did the shareholder's get the same results for the financial expenditure as compared to World War Two? Perhaps Iraq and Afghanistan will be leading allies with the USA in the years to come, perhaps the War on Terror sparked the 2011 "Arab Spring" leading to increased freedoms and liberties for those countries and perhaps these countries new leaders will embrace freedom and form new societies for their people. Perhaps not!

The question of freedom and the quest for democracy should come from within if it is to sustain. While we may not agree with our neighbor in the manner in which he rears his children, or maintains his home or in the quality of the food he eats, it is not a right from our creator for any one neighbor to barge into another's home, remove the household leader, alter the lifestyle of its household and train their children on our own way of life. Who provides the US with this power? On the other hand if we have a neighbor that beats his wife, allows poorly maintained lawns with weeds to infect our own laws, and are operating an illegal meth lab that may result in our demise should it blow; up or drives in a drunken stupor, we need to do something. The second passage of the Monroe Doctrine stated what the USA would do if an outside power attempted to move into the neighborhood and set up shop to the detriment of our great country.

> "We owe it, therefore, to candor and to the amicable relations existing between the United States and those powers to declare that we should consider any attempt on their part to extend their system to any portion of this hemisphere as dangerous to our peace and safety. With the existing colonies or dependencies of any European power we have not interfered and **shall not interfere**. But with the Governments who have declared their independence and maintained it, and whose independence we have, on great consideration and on just principles, acknowledged, we could not view any interposition for the purpose of oppressing them, or controlling in any other manner their destiny, by any European power in any other light than as the manifestation of an unfriendly disposition toward the United States."

In this key passage, however, it states that we "shall not interfere" with other neighborhoods outside our area of influence. Afghanistan military intervention by the USA most likely will go down in history as a just military action that came as a direct result of an attack on US soil. The Iraq military actions that will most likely end in a $1 Trillion price tab, in contrast to Afghanistan, may be subject to debate for years to come.

So what role does America play in global police force action? What about covert operations that drive influence in foreign countries? And finally, regime change, what role does America play in changing leadership in foreign countries and who pays for this? President Monroe, in his time-frame, most likely did not comprehend nuclear weapons or immediate threats from countries 4000 miles away.

Liberty and freedom, as discussed earlier, require continued investments to sustain our way of life. These investments should be designed to provide the most powerful deterrent with overwhelming consequences that would require pause even from the most obnoxious or mentally disturbed present day threat or gain respect from a growing potential threat.

1776 LLC EXECUTIVE MANAGEMENT TEAM

CEO: HEARN: "We are into this thing now for $1.3 trillion. We are going broke here, 9-10 percent of our workforce is unemployed and we can't seem to get the local governments and military infrastructure, in Iraq and Afghanistan, up to speed. I am not going to put another soldier in harm's way until I get some clear direction on what the hell is going on over there and how you guys are going to fix this thing. Where are we going, what are we doing, what is the strategy, who is going to pay for this, how do we communicate this police action effectively to the American shareholders? These shareholders' cannot continue on this path given the exorbitant debt they are now faced with and borrow money from one nation to support the drive of freedom in another. I understand the action in Afghanistan that costs the shareholders around $486 Billion. But Iraq; at $802 Billion, come-on now! World War Two only took 6 years. We're into these over 10 years and I we have no clue where this regime change experiment is headed. If we consider the interest on the existing investment of these two wars, alone, estimating the final tab of $1.7 Trillion, at 3% per year, that equates to $51 Billion a year in interest payments and given their existing ability to manage and pay down debt, we may be 10-15 years out before this debt is paid. We are talking about big dollars here, dollars we need to invest into share-holder growth."

VP HUMAN RESOURCES: BLACKWELL: "The shareholder's have varying opinions regarding the spread of democracy and preemptive strikes on rogue nations. The military is quite capable for these smaller campaigns and I question if the shareholder's will accept a simple "let's withdraw and go home strategy" given the history of our charter. Presently there are indications of future conflicts in North Korea and Iran and I think the shareholder's are tired of these campaigns especially given the present day enor-mous anxiety regarding their own economic salvation. If the shareholder's wish to pursue their role as the global police force then their military needs to be designed in such a way to act as police force and not simply trained as soldiers. If the shareholders are to pursue future regime change strat-egies they must be prepared to finance these as these are preemptive attacks with no cash in the treasury or budg-ets allocated. As the shareholders withdraw from Iraq and

Afghanistan will the Iraq and Afghanistan people reimburse the shareholder's for its expense in providing this freedom? Let's face it, the shareholders pay for the global police force. My concern is in line with our opening statements regarding planting the corn for a starving person, harvesting it for them and then leaving these persons to fend for themselves. As for the preemptive strike in Iraq, I fear that our charter is being redefined and I do not know if for the better or worse."

The management team has conflicting feelings regarding recent military actions, especially in Iraq and become increasingly uncomfortable with Blackwell's summary as it provides no solution to the financial impact; the purpose of the meeting.

BLACKWELL: I thank my colleagues in allowing me to monologue. We are here, however, to understand the decisions made by these shareholders, hold them accountable and attempt to bring some form of resolution. I feel the topic needs to expand from recent ten years of war in Afghanistan and Iraq and to the present day military models we have in place and how they will be managed and financed in the future.

VP BUSINESS DEVELOPMENT: GETHER: "John, let me start first with saying the investments made in Iraq and Afghanistan are considerable. Should the shareholders continue to pursue preemptive strikes and regime change strategies, than the shareholders should require their congress to provide a summary of financing for these strikes and method of payment prior to the investment of their precious soldiers and capital? It appears they have allowed for these recent wars with no strategy in place to finance the expenditures. Our growth initiatives outlined earlier will assist in increased GDP and tax revenues, but not significant enough to pay off the $15 Trillion debt of which these recent wars amount to about 11% of that debt. Afghanistan aside, the focus is more on Iraq, as this presents an interesting dilemma."

"With regards to reducing costs to pay down debt and raise capital for our growth initiatives, the business development guys see the present day military model as a target for significant costs reductions offset to a degree with investments. The shareholder's mindset apparently lies in the belief that fixed assets and deployment of trained military act as a major deterrent to rogue nations and larger countries preventing future conflicts and we are going to challenge that mindset."

"We need to look ahead 5-10 years to access what risks exist and formulate a more flexible and fluid defense structure with investments in technology and speed and less in higher fixed overhead costs that are chocking the shareholders. Do we really need 2 Billion square feet of owned and leased building structures? Do we need 150 Million square feet of buildings and related square feet in Germany and the UK?"

"Let's start first with the shareholder's military as compared with leading ten countries. Global Firepower published, under its Global Firepower List dated 7-10-2011 a summary of the leading 10 country military capabilities which I have summarized in Table No11."

Table No 11: Comparison of Top 10 Countries Military Investments

Rank	1	2	3	4	5	6	7	8	9	10
Country	USA	Russia	China	India	UK	Turkey	S. Korea	France	Japan	Israel
Active Military	1,477,896	1,200,000	2,285,000	1,385,000	224,500	612,900	653,000	362,485	239,430	187,000
Reserves	1,458,500	754,000	800,000	1,742,000	429,000	429,000	3,200,000	419,000	57,899	565,000
Land Weapons	56,269	91,715	22,795	75,191	11,630	69,774	13,361	10,261	5,220	12,552
Aircraft	18,234	2,749	4,092	1,663	1,663	1,940	1,568	1,757	1,953	1,964
Ships	2,384	233	562	175	99	265	170	289	1,110	64
Budget	$692B	$56B	$100B	$36B	$74B	$25B	$27B	$45B	$71B	$16B

" If you add up all the military budgets of the balance of the top 9 ranked countries it totals $379 Billion or 55% of the 1776 shareholder budget of $692 Billion."

"Nuclear capabilities are not included in the comparison as that study compared the investments by leading country for conventional warfare. Conventional war with Russia and China ranked second and third in military preparedness, would have global implications and we feel these two countries would prefer to maintain its boarders, at this time, with less aggressive growth activities as compared with 1900-1960. We further suggest that war with any of the balance of the top 10 nations is less likely than likely over the next 5-10 years leaving rogue nations as a potential for military engagement. The two nations that have been topics of conversation include Iran and North Korea. Assuming China would have a major problem with US military action that close to its boarders, it appears Iran is the only viable target. Iran ranked by Firepower.com as number 12 and North Korea ranked number 22 includes the following military investments outlined in my next slide; Table No 12."

Table No: 12 Military Ranking of Iran and N. Korea

Rank	12	22
Country	Iran	North Korea
Active Military	545,000	1,106,000
Reserves	650,000	8,200,000
Land Weapons	12,393	20,692
Aircraft	1,030	1,650
Ships	261	708
Budget	$9B	$5B

"We do not feel the 2.1 Billion square feet of US military fixed assets can address a nuclear war. It is more designed to address a conventional one, of which we feel is limited in scope over the next 5-10 years. A breakdown of the 2.17 Billion square feet of military controlled assets is summarized in Table No 2A

Table No: 12A US Military Use Overview by Square Foot

Purpose/Use	Total Square Feet(mill)	% Total
Operations and training	232	11%
Maintenance/Production	304	14%
Research and Development	69	3%
Supply	331	15%
Total Direct	**936**	**43%**
Hospital/Medical	58	2%
Administrative	232	11%
Family Housing	424	20%
Troop Housing/Mess Halls	263	12%
Community Facilities	236	11%
Utility and Ground improvements	22	1%
Total Support	**1,235**	**57%**
Grand Total	**2,171**	**100%**

Chris Murtagh

"I suggest the insurance premium the shareholders are paying is far in excess of its return and can be consolidated to a more effective one whereby we divest those overseas assets to the sponsor country, consolidate those assets on US soil and focus more on technological advances to address future conflicts. Jeff worked with me in developing a budget for this change and he will present the overview."

VP FINANCE: DARBON: "The purpose of this discussion is to find cost reduction areas to support the growth platforms we discussed earlier. If you recall we found close to $1 Trillion by redesigning the prison system with the military targeted to receive, train and rehabilitate these criminals providing initial cost reductions and ongoing savings outlined earlier in our discussions. This review provides a combined reduction in obsolete business models with investments in new technologies. In our "Grow America Campaign" we showed a total defense spending of about $820 Billion as compared to this military budget of $692 Billion. The budget I presented in The "Grow America Campaign" was for defense spending of which the military is the largest category the balance being other spending including homeland security and other smaller categories.

"The base divestment plan, outlined in my first slide summarizes the values we feel could be achieved by selling these assets to the host countries. The military values these at a replacement value, I suggest these facilities when occupied by the countries that purchase them, will provide significant value to those purchasers as opportunity value and have assessed that value at $400 per square foot for buildings and land. For sale of US assets, we propose $200 per square foot including land.

Table No13: Proceeds from Sales and Consolidation of Military Bases

Item	Quantity Square Feet	Year 1	Year 2	Year 3	Year 4	Year 5	Total
Square Feet	361,000,000	300,000,000	200,000,000	150,000,000	100,000,000	50,000,000	50,000,000
Sold		61,000,000	100,000,000	50,000,000	50,000,000	50,000,000	311,000,000
Proceeds		$24 Billion	$40 Billion	$20 Billion	$20 Billion	$20 Billion	$124 Billion
Consolidate US Operations	1,809,216,585	1,500,000,000	1,250,000,000	1,000,000,000	1,000,000,000	1,000,000,000	1,000,000,000
Sold		309,216,585	250,000,000	250,000,000			
Proceeds		$61 Billion	$50 Billion	$50 Billion	$0 Billion	$0 Billion	$161 Billion
Operating Costs	$4 per square foot	$1,480 Million	$1,400 Million	$1,200 Million	$200 Million	$200 Million	$4.5 Billion
Total proceeds							$290 Billion
Balance	2,170,216,585	1,800,000,000	1,450,000,000	1,150,000,000	1,100,000,000	1,050,000,000	1,050,000,000

DARBON: "We will reduce overseas facilities from 361 Million square feet to 50 Million square feet from 2012 through 2016 and consolidate US facilities from 1.8 Billion square feet to 1 Billion square feet over the next five years. Base operating costs, as outlined in an older version of the Government GAO report (General Accounting Office) in their 1996 report on military base closure showed a budget of around $25 Billion or $2 per square foot at that time. We inflated that to $4 per square foot (1996 -2011 inflation), supporting the base square feet at that time and we included that reduction, although smaller in its overall contribution, in operating costs for these facilities as well. In addition to these divestments and consolidations, we have already budgeted expansion plans in the "Cell Soldier" cost reduction initiatives outlined earlier that will most likely add to the square feet understanding those costs have already been accounted for in the "Cell Solider" campaign. We are looking at close to raising $300 Billion from this campaign.

MARKETING VP: BRINSTER: "Jeff, I don't mean to interrupt but let me understand this. You intend to replace the military with criminals, remove the greatest military deterrent by selling off and consolidating 50% of the military bases and expect the shareholder's liberties and freedom's will be defended appropriately. Is that what I am hearing? I mean, is that it?

VP R&D: THORPE: "Sounds revolting don't it? The last part of this initiative that I would like to call OBMD (Orbit Based Missile Defense) takes into consideration spending for technological advancements to provide for these consolidations and technology leadership. We will move from soldiers in the field and in the air to drones in the air and on the ground. Our military will include remote operated and computer controlled battle forces reducing the needs for the military forces, housing and fixed facilities following these change over the next 5 years. In addition, to address larger global or nuclear related threats, we intend on providing armed weapons in orbit that provide surveillance and defense potential. The criminals you spoke of will be in service for three years by the time we start introducing these new technologies and eventually back into the workforce by the time these new technologies are put in place. While it's difficult to assess, there are an estimated 6,000-8,000 drones in the military up from about 100 of them following the 9-11 attacks. The folks in Research and Development would like to see that number increasing to 30,000 drones over the next 5 years with equivalent ground force type drones used to replace conventional tanks. In addition to the actual numbers of drones, we will develop unique capabilities that allow access to historical ground force areas reducing fatalities of the soldiers. In addition we have assessed there are approximately 8,000-10,000 tanks that would be phased out and replaced with unmanned tanks controlled remotely. As we invest in these technologies, there will no longer be a need for local bases, brick and motor and associated overhead. "

"Following this transition from ground focused manned to unmanned military tactics, we will invest in more global deterrents by designing weapons and surveillance in orbit. We will not have that executed during the next 5 years but will be spending money on the design and development of these weapons over the term. We intend to have those completed in year 5 and move to install those in space from years 5 through 10. A summary of those costs are included in Table 13:

Table No: 13 Operation OBMD

Item	Quantity	Budget (ea)	Total
Drones	30,000	$500,000	$15 Billion
Remote controlled tanks	5,000	$1,000,000	$5 Billion
R&D Orbit Based Devices	100	$100,000,000	$10 Billion
Total OBMD Budget			**$30 Billion**

"We expect following these growth and debt balancing initiatives, to invest additional $400-$700 Billion in the OBMD program in years 6-12 once our economy is back on track and we are in a position to invest. We expect the normal phase in and phase out associated with these new technologies and will execute in parallel with base closings and consolidations.

VP FINANCE: DARBON: "I summarized these initiatives in Table No 14. Keep in mind gentlemen that we have a dual strategy here. We must make the investments Thorpe discussed in the future technologies for this OBMD plan to be realized in order to capture the shorter term gains in cash that we will use to invest in growth. In addition, it is critical that the military leadership discuss this in depth with the shareholders so they remain focused on the investments and, that changing political climates, do not discount these investments as they move forward. The shareholders need to be reminded that global peace comes with major deterrents and that these deterrents come at a high cost. It is that high cost in these deterrents that grant their freedom and liberty and way of life. I sense, in time, as world economies improve and the maturity of mankind increases, that a global police force guided by a set of international rules, supported by all nations, will eventually come into play-but do not see that for at least another 100-150 years."

Table No: 14 Summary of Cost Savings

Item	Investment
OBMD	$30 Billion
Building Consolidation	($290 Billion)
Shareholder Savings	**$260 Billion**

CEO: HEARN: "Sam you mentioned earlier that growth initiatives based upon technological leadership should not be the driving factor for change as the educational infrastructure is not up to the challenge, yet here you recommend a global orbit based defense system with surveillance technologies that have yet to be developed. What gives here?"

R&D: THORPE: "John, my observations were based upon strategic private sector growth initiates and not on cost reductions. In the case of the military, the shareholders have clear market and technological leadership both in weaponry and brain power. I feel more than comfortable in their ability to expand that expertise into new technologies and feel that they have already progressed down this road more than we know. As an example, the shareholders have unknowingly produced one of the leading military skill sets within its youth, required to support these initiatives, by providing hand held devices for their children manipulating computer based military warfare software entertainment games. These younger shareholders have been trained to use remote devices to fire weapons, control aircraft and kill enemies and have been doing so for the past 10-15 years. The hand held military games have been engrained in the shareholder children's capabilities and a critical area to support future unmanned tactics. Quite a fascinating observation! I further submit if a global rating of military warfare game for 15 year old shareholder children were rated on a global basis, as compared to its 14 rank in education, the shareholders would most likely lead in all categories including air, ground and sea assaults. In the case of military investments and technological leadership, the culture of warfare is strongly engrained in its shareholders down to the level of a 5-6 year old.

CEO: HEARN: "I like it. I like the idea of increased investments in technology coupled with reductions in outdated fixed overhead costs that, when combined, provide a greater defense arsenal at lower fixed costs. The shareholders will also see increased benefits in the private sector as they move from the technologies of the 1980-2000 to advanced technologies where they are already positioned against any other country."

Many agree that freedom, liberty and the individual's pursuit of happiness are critical components that define being an American. These differentiators however, come at a cost. Are preemptive *strikes and regime changes in the shareholder's benefit? During early days of World War Two the US shareholders wanted nothing to do with the war in Europe. The US provided over $50 Billion, prior to the US entry into the war, under its lend-lease act, in loans to Russia, Great Britain and a number of other countries to support their war efforts against an aggressive German dictator. The UK paid off the loans made in World War Two as recently as 2006. The understanding that freedom comes at a price expands beyond the lives lost during battle; it also requires financial resources and responsible management of the people's funds and trust. With regards to the strategy of regime change, where does this power come from? Who selects which country is to be changed and which is not? Are these powers provided by our creator? Do the shareholders get to vote on which regime is to be changed and which is not? What are the basic rules of engagement? What are the goals and objectives? In business the responsibility of investments and brand names weigh heavily on the management team as this team is responsible for its shareholder's funds and its ability to sustain the company. If its core competencies and brand name strength are in new innovative products and quality service, then it invests in those enterprises to sustain its growth. Freedom, liberty and the pursuit of happiness require economic security and a strong defense to sustain that vision.*

The threats of military action from smaller rogue nations appear on the radar scope now. Larger threats, however, loom in the distance. While America funds China to the tune of almost $3 Trillion in deficient trading since 1985 that deficient, if left unchanged, will most likely grow to $6 Trillion over the next ten years. Who is financing a new potential threat at their own demise?

Sun Tzu's Art of War, an ancient summary of warfare dating some time 700–400 BC summarized in "Attack by Stratagem "an observation of strategy to be employed by skillful leaders.

> "Therefore the skillful leader subdues the enemy's troops without any fighting; he captures their cities without laying siege to them; he overthrows their kingdom without lengthy operations in the field."

The OBMD initiatives along with unmanned ground tactics may provide a deterrent so powerful that future global conflicts may be avoided that subdue any enemy's troops prior to their deployment. 3 Billion square feet of real estate draining the treasury coffers appear to be yesterday's strategies. What about tomorrow?

CHAPTER 6

THE PRODIGAL SUM
$5,800,000,000,000

"Politicians say more taxes will solve everything...
and the band played on..."

—The Temptations (1970)

Overall government spending per resident in the United States has blossomed from $1970 per resident in 1970 to $19,354 per resident in 2010, with continued addiction to spending at a faster rate of population growth.

The number above, $5.8 trillion, is the dollars the local, state and federal USA governments spent in 2010 to support the American way of life. While there are slight differences based upon Republican or Democrat-controlled governments over the past forty years, it really doesn't matter. The system is out of control, and the spending is not in tune with the reality of the present-day USA population, or is it?

Let's take a peek at the largest categories of government spending and ask why these exist, what decisions we made along the way, and how we can learn from these decisions. Let's face it. The shareholders are responsible for the strength of the business. If the shareholders allow management to rape and pillage the business and do nothing about it, then the shareholders get what they deserve.

The overall growth in spending does not take into consideration inflationary increases that affect the percentage growth. These are actual dollars spent in those real days. More importantly, however, the data shows which programs were favored and received higher growth rates over the past forty years.

Table No: 15 US Government Spending ($Billions) 1970-2010 Federal, State and Local[18]

Category	1970	1980	1990	2000	2010	Growth
Defense	$95	$168	$342	$359	$848	793%
% Growth		78%	104%	5%	136 %	
Pensions	$31	$143	$305	$544	$939	2930%
% Growth		361%	194%	78%	73%	
Healthcare	$22	$87	$224	$470	$1028	4572%
% Growth		295%	158%	109%	118%	
Education	$56	$152	$305	$543	$887	1483%
% Growth		171%	78%	78%	63%	
Welfare	$22	$101	$175	$294	$727	3205%
% Growth		360%	73%	68%	147%	
Protection	$8	$24	$54	$193	$312	3800%
% Growth		200%	125%	257%	62%	
Transportation	$22	$57	$104	$167	$271	1132%
% Growth		159%	82%	60%	62%	
General Govt.	$7	$32	$56	$70	$111	1485%
% Growth		357%	75%	25%	59%	
Other	$36	$95	$234	$294	$382	961%
% Growth		164%	146%	26%	30%	
Interest	$19	$67	$234	$293	$296	1457%
% Growth		252%	324%	120%	1%	
Balance	$4	$14	$56	$13	-$4	(100%)
% Growth		250%	300%	-77%	-130%	
Total Spend	**$322**	**$940**	**$2100**	**$3250**	**$5800**	**1701%**
% Growth		192%	123%	55%	78%	
Population	**203**	**226**	**248**	**281**	**310**	**53%**
% Growth		11%	10%	13%	10%	

The largest growth categories (that make up 46 percent of government spending) from 1970-2010 include the following very vital and utmost important government programs that ensure the sustainability of the 1776 business model:

---

18   http://www.usgovernmentspending.com/budget_pie_gs.php?span=usgs302&year=2010&view=1&expand=&expandC=&units=b&fy=fy12&local=undefined&state=US#usgs302

1. Healthcare   +4572 percent
2. Welfare   +3205 percent
3. Pensions   +3930 percent

The lowest areas of growth from 1970-2010, reflecting the least important government spending programs, include:

1. Defense and Protection   +1026 percent
2. Transportation   +1132 percent
3. Education   +1483 percent

HEALTHCARE

The US shareholder spends approximately $8000 per year in healthcare spending as compared to leading global comparative countries including: France, UK, Germany, Canada and Australia ranging from $3000-$4000 depending on the country. Figure No: 23 outline these healthcare costs by comparative country and summarize the total expenditures as a per cent of their GDP. The Commonwealth Fund National Scorecard prepared its findings of these healthcare costs in its 2011 US Health Systems Performance Overview. The same rather extensive study, ranked the USA against its contemporaries in a number of critical areas where the USA received a score of 64% as compared to the Benchmark Rate.

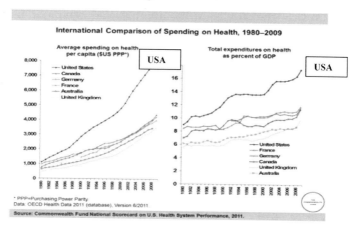

International Comparison of Spending on Health, 1980–2009

HEALTHCARE MARKET FORCES

The medical tourist industry is open for business and has not gone unnoticed by US healthcare insurers. This new industry provides airfare, hotel, modern equipment, world educated physicians, nursing staffs and many in facilities that rival any posh downtown hotel. In some cases, limousines are sent to the airport to pick up the patient and escort them to and from the hotels and hospitals for the required surgeries. Imagine getting treatment in a five star hospital, escorted to and from the hotel to the hospital by limousine and experiencing the highest level of customer service? Heck, last time I showed up for treatment I was left in a hallway and had to beg to get released from a local hospital 6 hours after I completed a routine heart stress test. Imagine private rooms with attentive staff and not have to wait endlessly for that pain shot? Market forces always have and always will drive change regardless of government intervention. A recent summary of select surgeries were compared by the national Center for Policy Analysis under their Study" Medical Tourism: Global Competition in Healthcare" where comparisons of cost were included in that report. Table No 16 summarizes those as follows:

Table No: 16 Cost of Medical Procedures in Selected Countries

Procedure	US Retail	US Insurer's Cost	India	Thailand	Singapore
Angioplasty	$98,618	$44,268	$11,000	$13,000	$13,000
Heart By-Pass	$210,842	$94,277	$10,000	$12,000	$20,000
Heart Valve Replacement	$274,395	$122,969	$9,500	$10,500	$13,000
Hip Replacement	$75,399	$31,486	$9,000	$12,000	$12,000
Knee Replacement	$69,991	$30,358	$8,500	$10,000	$13,000
Gastric Bypass	$82,646	$47,735	$11,000	$15,000	$15,000
Spinal Fusion	$108,127	$43,576	$5,500	$7,000	$9,000
Mastectomy	$40,832	$16,833	$7,500	$9,000	$12,400

1776 LLC EXECUTIVE MANAGEMENT TEAM

CEO: HEARN: "What the hell is going on here? We can't be spending all this stupid money, driving up our debt, and funding these programs. What has happened to our gross debt over these past forty years? These shareholders have got to be out of their minds. Let me attempt to put this in perspective, guys, and tell me where I am wrong. Following World War Two our economy, driven by a record level number of births defined as the "baby-boomers" starts to take off. Their debt as a per cent of GDP in the late 1940's is about 120% and they drive the debt down to about 25% of GDP in the early 1970's. Around 1973 they alter the lifestyle and start aborting these future shareholders in record numbers leading to a drop of some 50 million shareholders with an impact, considering children that should have been born, or around 70 million and still counting; basically wiping out the gains of the baby boomers. Women start entering the workforce in record numbers and men start reducing their numbers as a percent of available workforce. I estimate that more likely than not, these children left at home with lack of parental supervision start to decline in education and moral guidance that eventually leads to a decline in our education status and increase in prison rates. They then, around 1985 or so, decide it's in their best interests to export manufacturing jobs to China building up a deficient with China of almost $2.8 Trillion and reduce dependency in manufacturing one of the highest paid professions. Their workforce is aging, their population is aging and now they have allowed 10 million or so illegal immigrants in their country with local governments picking up the tab. Their infrastructure is crumbing and the highest investments as a per cent of growth are in the areas of welfare, healthcare and pensions and their lowest investments are in the areas of education, infrastructure and transportation. And I have a sense from the look on your faces that there's more we will discuss in the next few days. My question gentlemen is that while you have made bold and controversial recommendations to turn these phenomenon's around, do these shareholders have the fiber and gravitas to actually execute any meaningful bold plan and see beyond their own existence? I mean-come on now!

VP FINANCE: DARBON: "Sir, the public debt has ballooned to $14 trillion in 2010, up 2571 percent over the past forty years and they recently voted to increase it to almost $17 Trillion! Please refer to the overhead and my slide Table No: 17 and Figure No: 24 as discussion points."

Table No: 17 USA Gross Public Debts 1970-2010

Item	1970	1980	1990	2000	2010	Growth
Gross Public Debt	524	1,245	4,066	7,080	14,000	2571%
% Increase		137%	226%	74%	98%	

Chris Murtagh

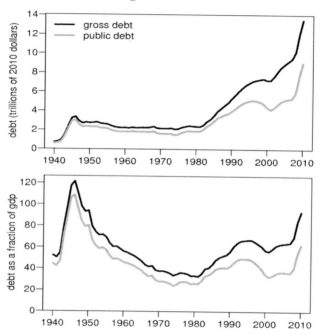

DARBON: The guys in Congress are looking at cutting expense programs, and the guys in the Senate are looking to raise taxes. They keep the game in play and use the TV as its worldwide audience to broadcast the circus. It's quite entertaining. The Democrats blame the Republicans for cutting out entitlement programs and scaring the shareholders that receive these entitlements to death by threatening to eliminate the entitlements from the less fortunate, and the

Republicans blame the Democrats for spending too much and for introducing these endless entitlement programs."

"This has been going on for years, as the shareholders suffer the consequences. The shareholders, however, seem unfazed, and I think they look to the government as a major form of entertainment as a break from their daily routines. These are a new kind of shareholder, most difficult to understand. On one hand, they complain about poor public school education and crumbling infrastructure, and then instead of investing heavily into these programs, they take 30 percent of the available funds and sink it into pension funds and welfare. Most have no clue on where the government is spending the money and do not invest time and energy on the topic because they feel it is overwhelming. The latest is a surge in television talk show hosts that point fingers and yell and scream at each other while the shareholders tune in at record numbers. Sir, if the shareholders do not drive the process, it is unlikely we can change it."

VP MARKETING: BRINSTER: "If I may, spending the shareholders' money recklessly, record deficits, rising the government spending ceiling, and placing the government in potential default on debt payments all point to the established disconnect the shareholders have with the administration. Our marketing studies show that most shareholders feel that Congress is out of control but eventually vote in people that keep the spending pattern in play. We try to communicate the importance of education and in investing in the infrastructure that helped define the 1776 business model, but the shareholders continued desire to put the decision-making into the government's hands is well defined by the spending patterns over the past forty years, and there appears to be no end in sight."

VP BUSINESS DEVELOPMENT: GETHER: "The shareholders lost sight of the original charter. The goal was to free hemselves from an intrusive government and to allow each shareholder to flourish based upon their own hard work and allow them to be enriched, with no limitations, based upon the freedom provided by and protected by the government. As the shareholders prospered, they allowed the government to intervene into the process, and rightly so in many cases, to help design an even and competent playing field for everyone. Let's face it; the Founding Fathers did a good job in the original design but left slavery on the table. Abe had to deal with that later in the game and eventually got the thing moving in the right direction. It wasn't until the focus on civil rights of the 1960s and1970s that eventually put certain entitlements into place and started the even playing field. We are still fifty to one hundred years away from putting that behind us.

"Unfortunately the intervention went to new levels, with decisions going a little too far and too many, and the cycle of dependence upon the central government body took new forms along the way.

"I feel a hard correction factor is due, and due quickly, as this 1776 business model continues to slow in its growth, increase its debt, and gamble the livelihood of the generations to come."

VP MANUFACTURING: YOUNG: "Guys, this is all good stuff, however, our infrastructure is crumbling, and our energy costs are out of control. Our pension funds are choking us, and our ability to compete on a worldwide basis diminishes daily. Our birth rates are down from the 1880s, we lost 50-80 million consumers through abortion and birth control in the past forty years, and we stay fixed on outdated educational and medical processes. Our ability to compete is less effective as time goes on, and we cannot get our cost structures in place. Our electric grid system loses 70 percent from point of generation to point of consumption, our medical records and lack of technological use increases our medical costs, our teachers still use the same books and classroom environments designed in the 1950s, where technology could replace all of that, and our infrastructure designed in the 1950s and 1960s no longer meet today's needs. Our workforce is aging, the shareholders are at record-level obesity, and our natural resources are shrinking. We need to make some decisions here, or we will not be able to compete effectively by 2030."

VP BUSINESS DEVELOPMENT: GETHER: "Okay, okay, I think we have all vented sufficiently here. If we make this mountain too tall, we will never get initiatives in place to affect a sustainable model moving forward. We do not want to kick the can down the road and delay the recovery by doing anything. Let me suggest we stay focused on supporting the growth and cost-cutting programs. So far our discussions and solutions address the previous decisions to reduce their future shareholders by importing 80 million new citizens. That will plug the consumer consumption gap and elevate GDP rapidly. In the case of manufacturing, we addressed an increase in the automotive industry of 50% over the next five years; that addresses the decisions of 1985 and reverses that quickly. In the case of cost reduction we addressed ineffective prison systems by terminating the present day prison business model and transferring that to the military. With regards to other cost reductions, we close ineffective military bases with high overhead costs and replace that with increased technology. We still have a ways to go with regards to other cost cutting measures, but all is not lost. I'd like to consider reducing costs associated with healthcare by reducing health care costs for those uninsured by exporting those for treatments to Thailand, Singapore or India and negotiating a deal where the shareholders could reduce medical expenses by 50% reducing government sponsored medical payments by $400-$500 Billion from its 2010 levels at $1.04 Trillion to $678 Billion by 2016. Based on what I read, they get a free trip to an exotic country; escorted with a private limo, stay at a jazzy hotel and use that time away for recovery. I'd like to see the shareholders reduce the spending pattern. Table No 18 on the overhead forecasts the budget savings."

Table No: 18 2011-2016 Healthcare Budget Forecast-Medical Tourism ($billions)

Item	1970	1980	1990	2000	2010	2011	2012	2013	2014	2015	2016
Healthcare Costs	$22	$87	$224	$470	$1028	$1080	$1133	$1190	$1250	$1312	$1378
		295%	158%	109%	118%	5%	5%	5%	5%	5%	5%
Annual Savings						$0	$200	$400	$500	$600	$700
Revised Healthcare Budget						$1080	$933	$790	$750	$712	$678
Cumulative Savings						$0	$200	$600	$1100	$1712	$2390

VP FINANCE: DARBON: Gentlemen, healthcare is the single largest overhead expenditure the shareholders have and it is growing out of control. After recent global ratings at 64% as compared to benchmark levels, spending at twice their contemporary's rates and a poorly orchestrated healthcare program resulting in poor global ratings, I would tend to agree and think we should call this one "broke and needs to be fixed". I suggest we present this one directly to the shareholders and assist in marketing these offshore healthcare capabilities directly to them, have the HMO guys jump in and promote lower rates to the employers for those that consider the advantage for the private sector and get the Medicaid and Medicare guys in government to start cutting deals. The impact will be devastating on the healthcare industry who receives payments from the governments but the destruction it is doing to our company far outweighs that special interest. Healthcare is an overhead expense and not a growth investment area. If we take the $2.3 Trillion and invest that money in schools, transportation and infrastructure, and the growth programs we presented earlier we get the shareholder's back on track. I think the shareholder's would prefer an exotic trip, limo ride and five star customer services.

VP MANUFACTURING: YOUNG: "I'm confused. We discussed the trade deficits with China in some detail and now we look to destroy another industry by exporting it to Thailand or Singapore? Assuming the quality issues of healthcare are similar to those of the USA and risks are minimal for the majority of services, the impact on the US healthcare system will be devastating.

VP MARKETING: BRINSTER: "These government, HMO and associated groups have screwed this thing up so bad that unless we address it head-on the shareholders will continue to suffer and the financial strain will continue to grow. I suggest that the remaining healthcare services left standing will be in far better shape than the healthcare industry is today. As I mentioned earlier-the government should not be competing with the private sector. When they do, these things happen. Unlike China that may be using unfair trade practices when shipping products into the US, these international healthcare providers are importing nothing. In addition they invested in leading technologies to move medical records at frightening speeds, do not have to compete with local foolish government regulations that destroy competition and provide lower cost advantage.

CEO: HEARN: "Ok. Thanks for letting me vent. It's frustrating to see this experiment called America in such a poor condition after all the investments in fortunes and lives to now see the shareholders in this poor frame of mind. We have been here before and we almost lost the whole damn thing during the Civil War. It's going to take another Abe or George style of leadership to put this on the table and level with the shareholders. They need a very sobering discussion on where they are and a clear plan of attack to remedy this. I feel we have provided a starting point, and I will listen carefully to the balance of the proposals"

VP BUSINESS DEVELOPMENT: GETHER: "I feel the majority of these issues are based upon a number of items including outdated business models, lack of shareholder interest, lack of their government services people educating the shareholders and lack of leadership at the highest levels. We need to convince their President and staff that these bold plans provide direction. If the shareholders are threatened by war they get focused, if threatened by disease they get focused. They need to understand clearly that an economic threat exists today and, if communicated effectively by sound leadership, these shareholders will get behind the growth plan. Our eventual goals are outlined in table No: 19:"

1776 GDP Growth Plan 2010-2016 $ In Billions
Table No: 19 1776 Five Year Growth Plan

Item	2010	2011	2012	2013	2014	2015	2016
Base GDP	$14,800	$15,096	$15,398	$15,859	$16,335	$16,825	$17,330
% Growth		2%	2%	3%	3%	3%	3%
1776 Growth Plan	$14,800	$15,096	$15,398	$16,561	$18,109	$19,713	$21,401
Grow America							
80 Million Consumers			$768	$768	$768	$768	$768
26 Million Cars			$78	$78	$78	$78	$78
26 Million Solar			$13	$13	$13	$13	$13
13 Million Homes			$195	$195	$195	$195	$195
Weed Out America							
New Consumption	$0	$0	$20	$50	$75	$125	$250
NOPEC							
24 Million Cars	$0	$0	$72	$72	$72	$72	$72
24 Million Solar	$0	$0	$12	$12	$12	$12	$12
OBMD	$0	$0	$5	$5	$5	$5	$5
Growth Initiatives	$0	$0	$1163	$1193	$1,218	$1,268	$1,393
Sub-Total			$16,561	$17,754	$19,327	$20,981	$22,794
Inflation-2%			$0	$18,109	$19,713	$21,401	$23,250

"The top 2 lines of this table outline what we see as the shareholders growth over the next 5 years given their existing debt burden, lack of clear growth plans and a continuing dependence upon reducing expenses and revising the tax structure; all non-growth and non-innovative in their design. 1776 replaces that lack of vision with bold and aggressive growth plans driving their economic growth at a pace of 10-12% per year by rectifying the shareholders past decisions, investing in transportation related growth and increasing technological investments in defense. We call this growth plan **Come-On! Cents.**

"I feel once these goals and growth initiatives are presented to the shareholders, they will get behind their leadership and look hard at the decisions made in the past. In addition to the growth plans, the cost reductions based upon changing outdated business models will provide the required funds to reduce the $15 Trillion debt in the same time period. We will provide a summary at the end of the meeting category by category providing the blueprint to the shareholders for their execution. The cost reductions will be summarized in the following presentations that, when combined with the growth initiatives will pay for the growth investments and reduce the national debt to zero in five years. In addition we project a significant increase in tax revenues that will provide for growth in infrastructure, education and defense all areas of least growth during the past 40 years.

VP R&D: THORPE: The medical industry, especially the doctor's themselves, tried to overcome many of these obstacles that keep the global industry rating so low. Many invested in privately owned surgery centers known as Ambulatory Service Centers or Outpatient Centers where the doctors themselves operated the business at a much higher customer service and efficiency rate as compared with hospitals. If I recall almost 75% of all surgeries in the US are now performed in these outpatient clinics. The actual costs for these surgeries, in many cases, are far below those of hospitals. Government intervention, however, required these businesses to hold patients less than 24 hours, ceased any personal referrals (allowed by any other normal business) and regulated the heck out of it. The government's position was that since the government was providing funding it would regulate. Why the government ever engaged itself it the medical business is beyond me. Many of these medical tourism packages are similar to the outpatient US doctor based ASC except with less regulations and increased focus on the business of healthcare. Why don't these government services guys invest in high tech medical information exchange, or other areas to lower these medical costs? I agree with the overall $2.3 Trillion proposed cost savings, but cannot align myself with imploding another US industry. Isn't there another way to fix this?

VP BUSINESS DEVELOPMENT: GETHER: Doubtful! Given its course and intervention from centralized government agencies along with increased foreign country competencies in healthcare reform, we will need to direct the shareholders down this path. It is unfortunate but continued meddling in private businesses has put the shareholders in an uncompromising position-one I fear requires immediate attention."

CEO: HEARN: "Thanks Gene. Ok this is starting to take form. We've already discussed reduced expenses with regards to the Cell Solider and OBMD programs and I am anxious to review the next areas of cost reductions. One question; you included in your summary 13 million homes as a GDP contribution-but these are more likely in place sales that are transaction based that do not directly affect the GDP per se for new products. What is the thought process here?

VP BUSINESS DEVELOPMENT: GETHER: "The effect of the growth initiatives goes far beyond what we are summarizing above. In the case of selling these in place homes, the new housing market will explode, home values will rapidly increase and bank balance sheets will become less burdened. Equity increases in the balance of existing homes owned, increases in new home sales and bank liquidity could easily double the $195 Billion a year projected in the growth plan but I wanted to capture the contribution in one form or another and did so in that manner.

CEO: "Ok, go it" Let' take a look at areas where these shareholders can reduce costs and redesign their business models more effectively so that we can provide the cash required to meet these growth plan objectives."

The numbers, by themselves, tend to tell a story. The story they tell is dependent upon the story teller and their interpretation of the historical information. The information suggests that money was given to the governing bodies by the shareholders. The governing body took the money, the shareholder's prodigal sum, and in their wisdom decided to spend the money in certain areas. The areas of highest spending increases are welfare, healthcare and pensions, all areas of overhead. Areas of investment including defense, transportation and education rated the lowest in spending increases. Come on now, America, can the shareholder's really blame the folks in Congress for selecting these vital programs and putting those in

Chris Murtagh

proper order? As the shareholder's continue to pilferage the coffers of their children and grandchildren to ensure pensions are protected, and their hearts keep beating until 132 years of age supported by whopping increases in healthcare spending along with public assistance checks rolling in, the questions concerning the crumbling transportation infrastructure and declining world ranking represented by the stellar public school systems (let the teachers eat cake) are left to fate. Is this is really America?

Now don't start getting patriotic with me, fellow reader. We all voted these guys in office, we all gave thumbs-up to the programs, and we all got caught up in a lack of "come-on" cents. And, hey, if you didn't vote or your guy didn't get in, it really doesn't matter. When spending was brought under control during any ten-year period, the next ten years, it simply jumps back to even higher levels. Let's face it: when the population grows over a forty-year period by 53 percent, and government spending grows at a rate of 1701 percent over the same period, we have moved from a capitalistic society motivated by market pressures to accelerate ourselves and our sense of less-entitled and more self-reliant performance, to a socialistic society where the care and burden of the shareholder's fellow citizens (see top three spending increase patterns) takes the place of preparing for their future citizens (lower three categories) for the future. Heck, screw em! As long as I have my pension, healthcare, and welfare checks rolling in, I'm a happy guy!"

Expanding growth and driving down costs requires the management team to review the economic condition of the company, understand where it has placed its investments and understand the culture of its society. The Soviet Union or USSR was created in 1921 and ceased to exist by 1992 after a 71 year attempt at a governing agree-

ment between countries. The European Union business model started about 1993 with its euro notes and coins replacing currency in its 12 member states in 2002. Recent economic issues with member countries in the EU are challenging that model. Economic security supported by competent business models require investment in growth areas and the responsibility to divest or change business models that do not work. It takes enormous maturity and strong leadership with vision that understands the decisions it makes today will reflect the economic returns of tomorrow.

The economy of a sovereign country is many ways identical to that of a business. Too many entitlements without the offset in ways to pay for these is irresponsible, hard cost cutting tactics that affect those challenged citizens is too brutal and lends itself to less education or medical benefits that eventually affect the sound business structure. A balanced approach combining bold and hard driving growth plans that the shareholders drove in their first 100 years of development, along with effective ways to pay for those defined the early 1776 economy. Lack of continued growth, with the highest per cent spending increases in welfare, medical and retirement benefits tend to define a culture of non growth and high investments in lower return areas that doom any business or any country.

Chris Murtagh

CHAPTER 7

I CAN'T ABILITY
$4,000,000,000,000

"Government's view of the economy could be summed up in a few short phrases: If it moves, tax it. If it keeps moving, regulate it. And if it stops moving, subsidize it."

Ronald Reagan

The 310 million shareholders look to their local, state and federal governments to provide for those services outlined in the Constitution that support a way of life that is the envy of most world countries. The charter, however, sometimes confuses the general public and its governments at the local, state, and federal levels. It looks to the government, from time to time, to intervene in areas where it should not. Through the years the shareholders have allowed their governments to get away from the job of governing and focus on investments in real estate, energy business, transportation and other areas where its government felt it was helping the shareholders or, at times of crisis, where only a centralized federal government could bring order or solutions to the problems of the day. These decisions many warranted and many politically driven in their nature, may be looked at from a different perspective. The shareholder allow for their governments to make an initial investment in non-governing areas, design the system or process to fix the issue of the day and then withdraw itself from these interests and convert those to the private sector or group of states, if warranted, and exit that business. An initial investment is one thing. A continued interest in spending the shareholders money to support an ineffective business or a business model that is better suited to the private sector is almost arrogant in its nature and taxes the liberty and freedom of its shareholders. By increasing the shareholder's debt and putting at risk shareholder capital that could be better utilized in growth strategies, these decision makers arguably are holding the shareholders hostage for predetermined agenda's that do not add to the welfare of the general population.

TENNESSEE VALLEY AUTHORITY

The Tennessee Valley Authority is a federal government owned non-profit power company. According to the Tennessee Valley Authority, 2010 10K financial filings, this utility company (TVA) generates approximately $11 billion a year in revenues against its electric generation of approximately 147 Billion kwHrs or approximately $0.07

per kwHr, pays no federal or state tax and employs approximately 12,000 workers. The TVA is the nation's largest electric power company, serving approximately nine million customers. The shareholders in the late 1930s felt it was the government's responsibility to go into the power business and sell electricity in Tennessee. History of the TVA is a controversial one where the local utilities felt it was irresponsible for the Federal Government to actually go into the utility business and complete with them, the Fed felt it was of critical importance to the region to invest a portion of the entire USA shareholder's funds in a certain region of the country to provide for local power and prosperity and at much faster rate than the private sector was able to do. In addition to the investment, approximately 50% of the power generated by the TVA comes from coal fired plants that provide 2.3 pounds of CO_2 emissions as compared to natural gas fired plants that emit about 1.3 pounds of CO_2 per kwHr. In addition comparable rates in the area are more in line with $0.07-$0.09 per kwHr so we have a government controlled power company that competes with local providers, does not collect federal and state taxes, operates one of the highest concentrations of coal fired plants and drives the market forces. Where in the constitution does it provide for this activity? Why is the government still in the power business? Can we divest this business and put the government back in the business of governing the country?

How much equity is tied up in this venture? How do we divest this business to the private sector, or should we?

What would the effect be and how can we take those funds and use them to grow the US GDP by 10-12% per year?

US POSTAL SERVICE

The postal service is a unique operating entity of the federal government and employed approximately 600,000 people in 2010. Revenues have declined over 29 percent from 1998 to 2008, and they are operating at a loss of $8.5 billion in 2010 with revenues of slightly less than $70 Billion. This government agency has a captive audience with the shareholders. Generally speaking, any business model that has a captive audience and is isolated from competition typically performs below the curve, lacks innovation, and does not lead markets. The UPS and Federal Express, as an example, have combined revenues of over $85 billion, and that opportunity was missed by this agency. The private sector continues to outperform this postal service, and with the postal service's continued declines in revenues due to e-mail and increased website and online use, it will eventually go the way of the dinosaur. Take a look at the 2010 figures:

Table No: 18 2010 Financial Summary Comparison

Item	US Post Office	Federal Express	United Parcel Service
Revenues ($Bill)	$67.05	$34.73	$49.55
Operating Income ($Bill)	-$8.5	$2.0	$5.87
Employees	596,000	141,000	400,000
Revenue $/Employee	$113,255	$246,312	$123,689
Income $/Employee	-$14,262	$14,184	$14,675

While the postal service played its role in the development of America, technology will continue to deplete the revenues as information exchange on the Internet replaces the common letter carrier.

Federal Express productivity per employee at $246,312 is slightly more than two times the productivity of the US Postal Service at $113,255 per employee. If the USPS could operate at the same productivity as Federal Express, it would reduce its employment by 50% or 298,000 people times $60,000 each would total $18 Billion in annual operating costs reduced.

Why is the Federal Government in the information transfer business in 2011? How much equity is tied up in these non-performing assets? Can we get out of these non-performing businesses or do the shareholders have to endure increased postage stamp rates, increased retirement benefits from retired postal workers, 50% productivity as compared to its largest private competitor? As the overall mailbox activity continues to decline, the Federal Government will now start to compete with the private sector and watch for declines in Federal Express and UPS revenues as this dinosaur business model, funded by the shareholders, creates a giant sucking sound. Does this make any sense?

NATIONAL RAILROAD PASSENGER CORPORATION AND SUBSIDIES (AMTRAK)

According to the Amtrak November 2011 "Monthly Performance Report for September 2011", financial statements table A-5.1, Amtrak, whose preferred stock is 100% owned by the US government, incurred losses of approximately $1.34 Billion ending September 2011 and are up from $1.309 Billion in losses from same period in 2010. The balance sheet shows Accumulated Deficient and Comprehensive Income of negative $29.9 Billion through September 2011 up from $27.19 Billion in the same period in 2010. By the way, The Passenger Rail Investment and Improvement Act of 2008 provides for five government grants to Amtrak that total $9.8 Billion from 2009-2013. Its on-time report declined slightly from annual 79.7% in 2010 to 78.1% in the same time period in 2011. The land and right of ways valued at $9.9 Billion is 89% of its total $11.07 assets. Amtrak has an estimated payroll of 19,000 workers.

The history of government intervention into private business sector goes beyond energy and transportation. As was the case with the Tennessee Valley Authority, the government services folks felt the best way to serve the public was to compete directly with the private sector, and to increase its investments in areas that do not make money and, in many cases, do not pay taxes at significantly reduced productivity.

Table No: 20 Comparisons of Two Railroad Companies

Item	Amtrak	Burlington Northern Santa Fe
Revenues	$2.7 Billion	$15.06 Billion
Expenses	$3.9 Billion	$11.00 Billion
Operating Income	($1.2 Billion)	$ 4.06 Billion
Employees	19,000	38,000
$ per employee	$142,105	$396,316
Accumulated loss	$29 Billion Loss	$25 Million Plus

REAL ESTATE INTERESTS

The federal government owns and operates approximately 70,000 buildings in the USA, estimated at approximately 3 billion square feet, according to the US Department of Energy's *Energy Data Book*. The GSA (General Services Administration), who maintain approximately 8300 of these buildings and manage a car pool of around 210,000 vehicles, employs around 12,000 federal workers at an annual budget of $26.3 billion and procures approximately $66 billion worth of goods to support this undertaking. Between managing the 8300 buildings and 210,000 cars, this annual expense amount is close to $100 billion a year.

Local and state government owned and operated real estate in the USA estimate approximately 11 Billion square feet of educational facilities, 4.8 Billion square feet of public assembly and countless prisons and other state and local government facilities whose operating costs and associated overhead are financed by taxpayer dollars. Ownership and management of real estate dilutes government growth initiatives and redirects investments from growth areas to supporting overhead operating costs. The Federal Government engaged in the electric power business and local governments engaged in the water supply and treatment business, wastewater treatment business, pose additional questions This debate will no doubt bring into play the services group that are not the does and thinkers who drive economic growth, but are the servicing arm of the business model that prefer to defend government's position as cracker jack real estate and business managers. Keep in mind that these government services groups have assisted in driving up pension growth over the past 40 years to the tune of 3930% as compared with education investments up only 1432% and transportation at 1132% over the same period. These numbers need to be reversed to sustain shareholder growth over the next 10 years.

If a business could be designed to sell these shareholder owned real estate assets to the private sector what would the return look like? Why does the City of Hackensack, NJ need to own a 100,000 square foot high school and manage it? Why? It can still provide education in a leased facility. Why lock up all that equity and cash that can be used to support growth initiatives or education investments instead of paying for the overhead required to support that?

1776 LLC EXECUTIVE MANAGEMENT TEAM

CEO: HEARN: "Ah, come on, now! What the heck is the government doing in these businesses? The balance of privately owned and operated commercial buildings in the USA is almost 80 billion square feet. There are private property management companies that can do a much better job and at lower costs than the shareholders can. There is so much equity tied up in these buildings and we need to divest these ineffective business models and invest in growth areas. And why are the shareholders in the electric power, utility and transportation businesses? They need to be in the business of growth supporting the private sector and not competing with it.

VP BUSINESS DEVELOPMENT: GETHER: "I mentioned earlier in the meeting that we could find the money for the recommended growth initiatives. This is just a sample of the equity sitting in building structures and older business models. The shareholders need to divest themselves from non-performing businesses, release the cash tied up in brick and motor, reduce the government employees hired to manage these assets and failing business models and invest it into growth programs. I suggest that the shareholders divest these business interests, sell them to the private sector and have their government services group focus on growth initiatives where the government can make a difference. Import new consumers, finance investments in transportation with the 50 Million electric cars along with cash for investment for solar power at the consumer level to provide energy for these electric cars, remove marijuana from prohibition status to a growth industry and pay for these initiatives by withdrawing from failing business models including prison systems that don't work, ownership in any industry that should be controlled by the private sector, divest itself from postal service industry that has been made obsolete, sell the underlying real estate and have it managed by the private sector reducing operating costs and government employees that are not focused on growth programs."

VP MARKETING: BRINSTER: "Selling these concepts to the shareholders may not be that easy. Special interest groups depend upon the shareholders ignorance of these matters and may attempt to blur the distinctions between services provided by these different entities and growth investments. I do not know why the Federal or local and state governments feel it needs to be on the energy industry, nor do I see any reason to keep the Federal Government in the business of delivering mail or operating railcars. These special interest groups are quite broad and deep and enter into endless areas of the private sector. The list goes on and on. I suggest a single slogan that states **"The government**

will not be engaged in any operating business that competes with any US private sector business interests". If we can put these government services guys back into the business of serving the does and thinkers and get them out of the way of actual business operations, the shareholders will be much better off."

VP FINANCE: DARBON: "Converting these non-growth assets into cash that will fund growth programs is the key objective here. I valued a number of these industries based upon present day investment criteria and summarized those as follows. My table also includes an offset in rental payments these government entities would have to make to maintain their space. My first slide, table number 21looks at the real estate holding and sells those to private investors.

Table No: 21 Real Estate Related Sales

Asset	Square Foot	Lease Payments	Investor Revenues	$ Value	Rent
Public Assembly	4.8 Billion	$24 per sq-ft	$115 Billion	$1.9 Trillion	$144 Billion
Public Schools	11 Billion	$24 per sq-ft	$264 Billion	$4.4 Trillion	$330 Billion
Total				$5.3 Trillion	$474 Billion
Discount-10%				($530 Million)	($47 Billion)
Total Proceeds				$4.8 Trillion	$427 Billion

"In addition to the sale of this real estate portfolio, we expect to reduce property management government personnel related to their upkeep by around 2% of annual revenues or $11 Billion a year.

Table No: 22 Sale of Energy and Transportation Assets

Asset	Revenues	Assets	Income (loss)	Value	Employees
Amtrak	$2.7 Billion	$11 Billion	($1.3 Billion)	$12 Billion	19,000
TVA	$11 Billion	$43 Billion	$1 Billion	$25 Billion	12,500
Post Office	$70 Billion	$60 Billion	($8.5 Billion)	$100 Billion	600,000
Total			**($8.8 Billion)**	**$137 Billion**	**631,500**

"Sale of these assets, in table number 22 assists in stopping the $9 Billion annual bleeding and support strengthening the private sector. In addition, it reduces government payroll by approximately 630,000 people and drives down future pension funds associated with government employees. The total contribution for these activities is shown in table number 23"

Table No: 23 Overall Proceeds/Annual Savings

Action	Proceeds	Annual Expense
Real Estate	$4.6 Trillion	$11 Billion
Outdated Business Models	$0.1 Trillion	$50 Billion
Total	**$4.7 Trillion**	**$61 Billion**

VP HUMAN RESOURCES: BLACKWELL: "Wow! I had no clue the shareholders were in so far and so deep. Wow! Just imagine if the government owned certain components of the airline, hotels and manufacturing industries or the auto industry (oops, sorry about the auto industry, I think they dabbled in that for a while as well). My concern here is that as the private sector acquires these businesses they would lay off about 300,000 people or so as they absorb these operations. In addition, what about the people that depend upon daily mail? Is this move forcing more online transactions? What about the people that don't own computers to complete their mail transactions? Won't the cost of a ticket for Amtrak eventually go up? Will the power costs in the TVA served areas increase?

VP BUSINESS DEVELOPMENT: GETHER: "For $8.5 Billion a year in the postal department related losses, the shareholders could purchase 17 million computers, at $500 each, to enhance information exchange; and that's 17 million computers a year! As for Amtrak if you include the accumulated losses at $29 Billion at an interest rate of 4% per year that equals $1.2 Billion per year in interest related debt alone or about 50% or their annual revenues. As for the TVA, these guys pay no taxes and have no competitors and more likely than not have kept prices below normal market rates. Regarding the 300,000 or so subject to layoff, we need every capable body to support the growth plans as we are forecasting unemployment at around 1% once these growth initiatives are put in place."

VP MANUFACTURING: YOUNG: "Stick to the knitting" a term made popular in Tom Peter's 1982 "In Search of Excellence" come to mind. The human resource components of this great charter basically include the doers, the thinkers and the support services groups. I like Brinster's catch all phrase: **"The government will not be engaged in any operating business that competes with any US private**

sector business interests". These support services groups including government, finance, legal, human resource services, educators and others; provide the even playing field and measure the activities of the doers and thinkers. By doing so, they provide a great service and keep the doers and thinkers on track. Once they cross the line and stray from the "knitting" under the guise of helping others and revert to taking over the doers and thinkers roles they start down a slippery slope of maintaining unprofitable business ventures or outdated business models at a great loss of productivity and freedom. I mean how does a private interest group compete with a government controlled entity that loses money, pays no taxes and has endless capital and resources available to them? Of increased concern is that these government controlled entities define the market levels and erode private sector investments in those market segments and eventually leads to poor performance. The private sector doers and thinkers are equally confused. Their recent entry in privatized education due to lack of performance by the service group educators has these shareholders all confused on what role they should be playing in keeping this charter focused. Get the government out of the transportation, energy, information exchange and real estate management business and get them focused on growth initiatives where they can really make a difference.

CEO: HEARN: "It appears you have identified around $4.7 Trillion in proceeds from the sale of these real estate and business units along with reduced annual operating costs of $61 Billion. The offset appears to be in increased lease expenses of around $427 Billion per year to outside investors. We are going to need that cash to support the growth programs to meet the target $25 Trillion GDP by 2017. I think we have enough to put together the 5 year Come-On! Cents strategic plan. Good job, guys. Let's summarize this tomorrow and prepare the plan for release next month.

Some companies are too big to fail. Some countries are also too big to fail, but both do. Pan Am airlines, started in 1927 was liquidated in 1991. It owned hotels, one of the largest commercial buildings in New York City and through a number of reasons, blamed on mismanagement, is now gone. In 1971 Southwest Airlines, with its finger on the pulse and an understanding of what consumers valued in air travel, propelled itself to a leadership position in about half the time it took Pan Am to fail.

Some companies have the ability to reinvent themselves to meet changing conditions. Some don't. Successful companies tend to measure the performance of their businesses based upon profitability and in meeting with its long term growth and ability to sustain planned growth. Many stay engaged in certain businesses that do not appear profitable but support their longer term growth strategies. At times they hire outside consultant groups to provide a third party perspective of their assumptions and risks to ensure the management team is not caught up in its own internal values or culture when making these strategic decisions. A company, however, with endless resources, limited competitors, obnoxious losses, staggering debt that remains engaged in non-performing businesses that taxes their balance sheet and undermines the growth of private sector businesses is an entity to be feared as it eventually has to pay the piper for it arrogance.

CHAPTER 8

$27,000,000,000,000 GDP

The national budget must be balanced. The public debt must be reduced; the arrogance of the authorities must be moderated and controlled. Payments to foreign governments must be reduced, if the nation doesn't want to go bankrupt. People must again learn to work, instead of living on public assistance.

—Marcus Tullius Cicero, 55 BC (106-43 BC)

CEO: "Guys, this strategic planning session was worthwhile. We studied the markets, took a look at where we are spending the 305 million shareholders' money, and developed a set of plans to improve the business and provide increased shareholder returns. We need to throw out certain plans that this shareholder group is not capable of executing and focus on those plans where we feel this group of shareholders has the ability to get behind those and execute effectively."

VP MARKETING: BRINSTER: "Thanks John. Prior to the discussions on what to and what not to execute, I thought

I would summarize the condition of our 1776 charter in a brief SWOT (Strength, Weakness, Opportunity and Threat) diagram that we can all "talk to" in an effort to ferret out those plans that we can actually execute and those that we want to hold for now. I prepared Figure No 25 as an overview:"

Figure No: 25 1776 LLC SWOT Analysis

- Freedom
- Liberty
- Lifestyle
- Defense
- Shareholder Values
- Strength

- Management
- Growth
- Education
- Manufacturing
- Welfare
- Debt
- Deficiets

Strength   **Weakness**

Opportunity   **Threat**

- Market
- Share
- Energy
- Business Design
- Growth
- Educate Shareholders

- China
- Shareholder Values
- Services Group
- Aging Population
- Debt

"We need to balance these plans with the understanding of the SWOT analysis. The opportunities that we outlined in these growth plans will be offset with weaknesses within the shareholders structures. We defined the services group (government, legal, education and finance) as threats to the business model as many of these services need to be redirected to support and not lead economic recovery. These same services group have not addressed the manufacturing imbalance with China, nor have they addressed their desire to invest in outdated business models or invest in business models better serviced by the private sector. As a result our execution plan needs to address that lack of ability (management weakness) to ensure we do not plan too aggressively in those areas."

VP BUSINESS DEVELOPMENT: GETHER: "Based upon your outline, I suggest we drop the "Cell Solider, Healthcare and OBMD" initiatives as these are fully controlled by the government services groups and regardless of the short term and longer term misdirection, they will not have the capability to resolve those especially given such a short time frame. I fear their lack of attention to this matter will continue to erode their future investment decisions. I do fell however, that the "Weed-Out America" program has merit and will reduce the prison population associated with marijuana and increase employment and tax revenues to the government. In the "NOPEC" initiatives, this is less of a government services as compared to the doers and thinkers ability to gather the workforce and execute the plan to build additional 24 million cars with associated solar power collectors installed in the homes of those recipients."

VP MANUFACTURING: YOUNG: In addition to these growth strategies the issue of trade imbalance with China needs to be pursued. While we discussed the impact of its $2.8 Trillion deficient with China since 1985, we did not come to any resolution. Given that I traditionally do not like the idea of imposing trade barriers or having trade wars, there are, at the same time compelling issues that need to be resolved. If there are improper practices by China that are well documented then that imbalance should be resolved. I understand that this area of management capabilities for the shareholders is defined as "weak" it must be addressed as we would then loose these 50 million new electric vehicles to China manufacture and further engage the shareholders in additional trade deficits that have been too long overlooked and that is the worst possible thing that could happen. As much as I despise the controls, I must suggest that the growth initiatives be guarded from the government services group that will either over regulate these initiatives or expedite their export to foreign countries that will cause the inevitable failure of 1776 LLC. I fear without these controls, we put the shareholders in a terrible position. I agree with Brinster and Gether that we do not pursue savings in the defense and prison systems as both of these historically depend upon the government and they are not in a position to change their culture during the next 5-7 years given all that will be on their plate.

VP R&D: THORPE: I like the concept. Reduce the growth strategies to those that add value to the highest degree in the US that include manufacturing and construction, stay away from political charged agendas and look to areas of cost reduction that are simpler in their nature to execute. I would like, however, that these cost reductions and growth initiatives allow the shareholders to rapidly increase expenses in education and infrastructure during these growth years as these two issues will lead to the following five year growth plan as the population nears 400 Million by 2017. I agree with Gether that the "Weed Out-America" program will assist in immediate reductions in prison time in the short term. Significant increases in education budgets will reduce the longer term if the shareholders have the personal values and commitment to invest there and if the services group have the ability to change to a more enlightened educational process and move from the 1950's agenda to a modern environment education structure that leverages technology in the classroom. I feel if the investments and direction are there, both groups will respond.

VP BUSINESS DEVELOPMENT: GETHER: "Darbon helped me summarize the growth initiatives and cost reductions planned based upon excluding the Cell Solider and OBMD programs as the team feels the shareholders do not have the capabilities to execute those latter two programs. In addition the team feels that by executing the Weed-Out America plan and investing in new education reform, it will have a significant short and longer term effect.

CEO HEARN: "The more consideration I give the SWOT analysis the more concern I have that these shareholders will be able to sort out the marijuana related issues and any issue controlled by government that affect the social lifestyle, including the post office. I agree on the sale of anything that competes with the private sector including railways and power companies. I know I'm throwing you guys a curve here, but any group of shareholders that have allowed for this level of debt cannot possibly execute so many of these initiatives in such a short period of time. Perhaps they can experiment with some of these, but let's not plan on their actually executing those over the next five years. Given those exemptions, Jeff, what do we have here?

VP FINANCE: DARBON: "I summarized the existing shareholders plans, excluded those you just mentioned and placed for consideration the growth plans, cost reductions and recommended investments in a series of slides that I would like to present. Table No: 24 for your consideration is titled "Come-On! Cents 2012-2017 strategic plan and includes additional revenues from construction actives not included in the baseline plan that are needed to expand the infrastructure to support the new 80 million residents. Baseline building types and square feet are in place existing structures that will need to be expanded. The contribution from the construction industry is in Table No: 24

Come-On! Cents Five Year Strategic Plan
2012-2017 Term
"Grow America" Private Construction Impact: 5 Year Term
Table No: 24

Plan	Building Type	Existing Sq-FT	Growth	Needed Sq-Ft	Cost PSF	Construction	Employment
Grow America	Education	11 Billion	26%	2.86 Billion	$200	$572 Billion	1.9 Million
	Manufacturing	12 Billion	26%	3.10 Billion	$150	$465 Billion	2.1 Million
	Medical	7 Billion	26%	1.82 Billion	$500	$500 Billion	1.2 Million
	Retail	13 Billion	26%	3.38 Billion	$150	$507 Billion	2.3 Million
	Lodging	6 Billion	26%	1.56 Billion	$300	$468 Billion	1.1 Million
	Total	**61 Billion**		**12.72 Billion**	**$198**	**$2,512 Billion**	**8.6 Million**
	Per Year						**1.72 Million**

"The shareholders will need to add 1.5-2 Million new construction workers per year over the five year period to meet the expansion plans required to service the 26% growth from these new 80 million residents planned. This is incremental to other typical expansions and needs to be planned accordingly.

"Table No 25, my next slide, summarizes the impact of each of these growth initiatives by major category and summarizes increased employment above and beyond the construction employment associated with expansion plans. I captured the impact by growth strategy and summarized the employment impact.

"Grow America" Employment Impact 5 Year Term
Table No: 25

Industry	Present Day	Growth Population: 26%	Auto Industry 50 Million Employment	Construction Grow America	China Trade $300 Billion	Solar Business	Total Impact	% Increase
Total Citizens	310,000	80,000					390,000	26%
Workforce	154,198	26,000					180,198	17%
Unemployed	13,900						-4,484	
Unemployment Rate	9%						-2%	
Construction	5,525	1,437	75	1,720	1,100	500	10,356	87%
Manufacturing	11,759	3,057	1,200	0	2,000	100	18,116	54%
Mining/Logging	810	211	0	0	25	0	1,046	29%
Service Sector	91,443	23,775	800	1,150	1,000	40	118,208	29%
Government	21,979	5,714	0	0	0	0	27,693	26%
Total non-farm	**131,516**	**34,194**	**0**	**0**	**0**	**0**	**175,419**	**33%**
Agriculture/Other	8,782	2,283	0	0	0	0	9,065	3%
Unemployed	13,900						(4,484)	
Total	**154,198**	**36,477**	**2,075**	**2,870**	**4,125**	**640**	**184,484**	**20%**

"The new 80 million residents include 26 million working adults and 54 million children, given our plan of 6 per household outlined earlier in our discussions. The growth in the available workforce increased by 26 million but we need 30 million workers to meet the expansion plans from available workforce today of 154 million workers to 184 million needed. We move from a 9% unemployment rate to a negative 2% unemployment rate. I suggest they legalize their 10 million or so illegal aliens and include 4-5 million of those to plug the gap in employment needs. These illegal aliens are already supported by their existing infrastructure and I would expect to see some increases in these baseline growth numbers once they move from "illegal" to "legal" status, but not to the same extent."

"We have not assessed the impact on public construction including sewers or water supply since the 13 million homes targeted are already in place and serviced by utility companies and infrastructure. The concern is when new housing and 3 trillion square feet of non-residential comes into play during this five year growth plan and prefer to look at those as a consequence to the growth with local states providing historical infrastructure financing as they had in the past. We also assume the expansion at the manufacturing level are absorbed by US manufacturers and not exported to foreign companies.

"Finally, in Table number 26, I summarize the adjusted GDP based upon these agreed upon growth initiatives.

Come-On! Cents Six Year Strategic Plan
2012-2017 Term
Revised Growth Plan $27 Trillion
Table No: 26

Item	2010	2011	2012	2013	2014	2015	2016
Base GDP	$14,800	$15,096	$15,398	$15,859	$16,335	$16,825	$17,330
% Growth		2%	2%	3%	3%	3%	3%
1776 Growth Plan	**$14,800**	**$15,096**	**$15,398**	**$17,684**	**$20,016**	**$22,486**	**$24,915**
Grow America							
80 Million Consumers GDP			$768	$768	$768	$768	$768
26 Million Cars			$78	$78	$78	$78	$78
26 Million Solar			$13	$13	$13	$13	$13
13 Million Homes			$195	$195	$195	$195	$195
Commercial Construction			$502	$502	$502	$502	$502
NOPEC							
24 Million Cars	$0	$0	$72	$72	$72	$72	$72
24 Million Solar	$0	$0	$12	$12	$12	$12	$12
China Reverse Imbalance			$300	$300	$300	$300	$300
Growth Initiatives	**$0**	**$0**	**$1,940**	**$1,940**	**$1,940**	**$1,940**	**$1,940**
Sub-Total	**$14,800**	**$15,096**	**$17,338**	**$19,684**	**$22,046**	**$24,426**	**$26,855**
Inflation-2%	**$15,096**	**$15,398**	**$17,684**	**$20,106**	**$22,486**	**$24,915**	**$27,392**

CEO: HEARN: "Thanks Jeff. I follow the summary and GDP impact. I think by capturing the hard costs for construction and not the land and soft costs gives us a little upside to the numbers. I also think that by focusing these shareholders at end user level for solar power may contribute to lowering solar power manufacturing costs and increasing shareholder private investments in that area that they may benefit from in the future. The China trade imbalance is an area of immediate impact and I agree that this initiative is manageable and can be executed by these shareholders. Auto, construction, manufacturing are areas of growth where these shareholders have the capabilities and desires to achieve greatness. I feel they will get behind the growth plan and push the services group folks accordingly.

VP FINANCE: DARBON: If the team is OK with what I have presented, then I'd like to proceed with the summary that outlines the costs to execute these plans and how we are going to pay for it. Table No: 4 summarize the growth initiatives we all agreed upon and the costs to execute those plans. In addition, I captured the annual savings from associated overhead that is reduced and will become a portion of the debt reduction strategies that will follow these steps. Table Number 27 outlines the cost of these indicatives and the source of revenues to pay for these:

Come-On! Cents Six Year Strategic Plan
2012-2017 Term
Cost of Growth Plans $3 Trillion
Table No: 27

Item	Budget (ea)	2012	2013	2014	2015	2016	Total
Grow America							
13 Million homes	$75,000	$195	$195	$195	$195	$195	$975
26 Million Cars	$30,000	$156	$156	$156	$156	$156	$780
13 Million home solar	$2500	$6.5	$6.5	$6.5	$6.5	$6.5	$32.5
NOPEC							
24 Million Cars	$30,000	$144	$144	$144	$144	$144	$720
24 Million Solar Collectors	$2500	$12	$12	$12	$12	$12	$60
Total Government Costs		$514	$514	$514	$514	$514	$2,570
Leased Real Estate		$71	$142	$213	$284	$355	$427
Total Costs		$585	$656	$727	$1,011	$1,366	$2,997
Sale of Real Estate		**$585**	**$656**	**$727**	**$1,011**	**$1,366**	**$2,997**
Balance		**$0**	**$0**	**$0**	**$0**	**$0**	**$0**

"Sale of the real estate assets alone will provide the $3 Trillion in initial outlays. Available $4.8 Trillion of real estate sales gives the plan a $1.8 Trillion cushion and maintains off-setting real estate lease payments of $427 Billion per year. We have the cash to invest in these limited initiatives. I did not include any "buy-backs" from the previously outlined strategies for the 50 million cars issued and for the homes purchased from the banks. Those combined incentives totaled $562 Billion and I suggest we give that flexibility at the state level to offset their annual lease payments during the growth phase. Total lease payments on sales of the real estate totaled $427 Billion over the term and will remain at that level until they either purchase back the real estate of levy taxes to offset the costs. Given zero unemployment and increases in GDP, there are more than sufficient funds to pay for those leases over the term. My final slide, Table No: 28 summarize the national debt and balance at the end of the fifth year."

Table No: 28

Item	2000	2010	2011	2012	2013	2014	2015	2016
Base GDP	$9885	$14,550	$15,079	$17,684	$20,106	$22,486	$24,915	$27,392
Total Government Spending								
Defense	$359	$848		$700	$575	$500	$450	$400
Pensions	$544	$939		$975	$1004	$1034	$1000	$950
Healthcare	$470	$1028		$1090	$1123	$1157	$1191	$1226
Education	$543	$887		$900	$945	$1020	$1071	$1124
Welfare	$294	$727		$750	$725	$700	$500	$300
Protection	$193	$312		$250	$240	$225	$200	$180
Transportation	$167	$271		$290	$295	$300	$275	$260
General Government	$70	$111		$100	$100	$100	$100	$100
Other	$294	$382		$275	$270	$250	$240	$230
Interest	$293	$296		$300	$305	$275	$265	$250
Total Spent	$3500	$5800		$5630	$5582	$5561	$5292	$5020
% GDP	40%	39%		32%	28%	25%	21%	18%
Total Tax Revenues	$3513	$3767		$5534	$6293	$7039	$7898	$8573
State Tax Revenues-10%	$1000	$700		$1768	$2011	$2249	$2592	$2739
Local Tax Revenues-6.3%	$630	$905		$1114	$1267	$1417	$1569	$1725
Federal Tax Revenues-15%	$1883	$2162	$2302	$2652	$3015	$3373	$3737	$4109
Surplus (deficient)	$13	($2033)		($96)	$711	$1478	$2606	$3553
Federal Debt			$15,000	$15,096	$14,385	$12,907	$10,301	$6,748
Federal Debt % GDP			100%	85%	72%	57%	41%	25%

"We have not achieved the goal of eliminating the debt but have reduced the debt as a per cent of GDP from 100% in 2010 down to 25% in 2016, reduced overall government spending from 40% of GDP in 2010 down to 18% in 2016 and have used the surplus to pay down debt. This will require the shareholders to provide an amendment to its constitution for the Federal Government to balance its budgets each year. If we can convince them to provide partial execution in reduced spending and adopt several of the healthcares, cell solider and exit private sector businesses, I feel the Federal spending can be curbed by about $300-400 Billion a year. That amounts to almost $2 Trillion in five years bringing the debt down to $4.7 Trillion or 17% of GDP. The decline in the federal debt will require the fed to allocate its existing debts to each state as the states are providing the investment cash. The states will pay off the federal debt over the next five years and hold the feds to a strict and balanced budget and return economic freedoms back to the states and to the shareholders.

CEO: HEARN: "I agree with the thought, but these initiatives do not allow for "half pregnant" execution. It would only fail. With regards to the forecast budgets, they may disagree with your allocations, but I feel we accomplished the goal of providing a growth plan for the shareholders to get them focused and make the necessary investments in their future and the future of their children. Gentlemen, please give me a brief summary of your thoughts. I'd like to present this summary to the shareholders sometime in early 2012 and get them challenged and engaged in their future and the future of this fine company, 1776!

Can we summarize where we see these historical shareholder decisions made and their impact that allows the team to communicate more effectively in changing their behaviors and get the country back on track? Gene, can you pit these in some order?

VP BUSINESS DEVELOPMENT: GETHER: "Attached is our summary slide. The slide suggests that almost 60% of the $15 Trillion Federal debt is associated with shareholder decisions that could have been avoided if growth and investment outweighed overhead and old business model designs. The largest contribution to the overall debt is the shareholder's desire to reduce their future consumers; and that falls directly on each shareholder and not on the government services or any other party. Table 29 summarizes our observations.

Table No: 29

Topic	Shareholder Decisions	Quantify	Lost GDP	Tax Impact	Federal Debt
Grow America	Reduce future shareholders	80 Million	$45 Trillion	$13.5 Trillion	$6.8 Trillion
China	Approve Trade deficit	1985-2010	$3.0 Trillion	$0.90 Trillion	$0.5 Trillion
Wars	Approve Iraq War	10 Year War			$0.5 Trillion
Business	TVA/Amtrak/Other	Losses			$0.3 Trillion
Models	Tolerate Postal service/other				$0.4 Trillion
Total			**$48 Trillion**	**$14.5 Trillion**	**$8.5 Trillion**

1776 LLC management team has approached its Charter with a number of new ideas and concepts, many of these bold and many that are outright ridiculous. In a disastrous business climate with no clear goals in sight, the only ridiculous idea is the one never presented. Corporations challenge their business models constantly; they are required to defend areas of expense where there appear little or no returns, divest businesses where they can no longer compete effectively and focus on areas of investment where they feel its own business culture and its core competencies can gain an advantage over its competition. It also establishes an overhead budget and financial metrics that guide its decisions, requires innovative changes to business models to reduce operating expenses and drives to add value and communicate that value added to its shareholders. Respect for its shareholders combined with the culture of an experienced management team is critical components to sustaining any business. The arrogance, however, of any management team that feels it is entitled to lose its financial strength by staying focused on failing business models, or not communicating critical information required by the shareholders to access its situation is not only poor business climate but downright illegal for most public companies. Transparency at the highest levels of leadership sets the proper example. The shareholders, however, that tolerate poor returns, or tolerate lack of clear communications allow for irregular or improper management behaviors and are ultimately responsible for the results. It is and always has been the shareholders responsibility to stay informed to allow for prudent decisions.

1776 management team has discussed a wide number of solutions yet understands its shareholders are responsible for the current situation that did not happen overnight. Once the shareholders hold themselves accountable, as a group, and not act as simple victims whose future are determined by fate, the situation will be resolved. Unfortunately for Americans the gift of liberty, freedom and the right to pursue happiness holds each of us at a much higher standard as compared to our global contemporaries. We know what it means to be free, we know what it means to have liberty and all of us know the pursuit of happiness or at least the right to pursue it; that's why we are here.

What is wrong with challenging the norms? Why should the government services groups require that the shareholders own railroads, power companies or anything else that dilutes their ability to govern? Why is it that a 12 year old junior high school student can design a personal website, download pictures and events at lightning speeds, have hand held phones that speak to them but can't learn excel or PowerPoint in the sixth grade? Why is it that the US Postal Service, fighting a losing battle against technological advancements, continues to lose Billions of our taxpayer dollars each year in order to deliver mail that, for the most part, is thrown away and continues to pollute the landfills? Why do we continue to bleed the treasury by enslaving our fellow shareholders in a failing prison system for smoking or engaging in the use of marijuana when right across the street at a local tavern, other shareholders have the rights to inebriate themselves? Why do we export our manufacturing to China and cripple our fellow workers driving them to unemployment while we watch our economic systems collapse? And why do we continue in the practice of disposing of our future citizens with the observation that we have the right to do so?

A recent movement in the USA called "Occupy Wall Street" came about during the writing of this book. Its future and impact are still under scrutiny and may be a past phenomenon when this book is eventually published. It is, however, an example of shareholder's civil liberties to communicate a voice, a voice of frustration and a voice that desires change. These same voices defined America's experiment and are responsible for many changes it *its 235 year history. It is the voice of the American shareholder that is the most feared in the world as it transcends inept governments, greedy businesses, and poor business models and will eventually lead the American shareholder to force change. In its civil disobedience, respected by the world, the 1776 shareholder is to be feared. Once they have direction and a common purpose, these shareholders will evoke change on a global basis. I trust Come-On! Cents has challenged those progressive enough to drive change and not wait for it to come.*